The Princeton Review.

CRASH COURSE
for the ACT®

5th Edition

Shawn Michael Domzalski and
the Staff of The Princeton Review

PrincetonReview.com

Penguin
Random
House

The Princeton Review
24 Prime Parkway, Suite 201
Natick, MA 01760
E-mail: editorialsupport@review.com

Copyright © 2015 by
TPR Education IP Holdings, LLC.
All rights reserved.

Published in the United States by
Penguin Random House LLC, New York,
and in Canada by Random House of
Canada, a division of Penguin Random
House Ltd., Toronto.

ISBN: 978-1-101-88169-9
ISSN: 1546-0614

ACT is a registered trademark of
ACT, Inc., which does not sponsor or
endorse this product.

The Princeton Review is not affiliated
with Princeton University.

Editor: Meave Shelton
Production Editor: Kathy G. Carter
Production Artist: Fishbulb Design

Printed in the United States of America
on partially recycled paper.

9   8   7   6   5   4   3   2   1

Fifth Edition

Editorial
Rob Franek, Senior VP, Publisher
Casey Cornelius, VP Content Development
Mary Beth Garrick, Director of Production
Selena Coppock, Managing Editor
Meave Shelton, Senior Editor
Colleen Day, Editor
Sarah Litt, Editor
Aaron Riccio, Editor
Orion McBean, Editorial Assistant

Random House Publishing Team
Tom Russell, Publisher
Alison Stoltzfus, Publishing Manager
Melinda Ackell, Associate Managing Editor
Ellen Reed, Production Manager
Kristin Lindner, Production Supervisor
Andrea Lau, Designer

Acknowledgments

I would like to thank my editor, Ellen Mendlow, for being so supportive and for asking me to work on this project (and many others), and Bill Lindsley, who encouraged me to focus my energies on learning all there is to know about the ACT and who has provided wise counsel on more than one occasion. And thanks to David Kwok for allowing me the time necessary to complete this project while working in The Princeton Review's LA office as well.

Thanks to Chris Dent for his careful revision of this book.

Also, thanks to the fine folks at ACT in Iowa City, without whom there would be no ACT.

Finally, thanks to Danielle, for the love, the support, the strength, and the friendship. You rock.

Special thanks to Adam Robinson, who conceived of and perfected the Joe Bloggs approach to standardized tests and many of the other successful techniques used by The Princeton Review.

The Princeton Review would like to thank Jonathan Chiu, National Content Director for ACT, and Kathryn Menefee for their careful revision of and contributions to the fifth edition of this book.

Contents

PART I

Introduction

Orientation

Orientation

What Is *Crash Course for the ACT?*

Crash Course for the ACT is the book to buy if you don't have a lot of time to prepare for the ACT and want to spend what little time you have as wisely as possible. Simply put, this is a focused review of what you need to know for the ACT. The techniques and drills contained in this book are all intended to help raise your score. This is not a comprehensive review of the ACT; for that, you should get The Princeton Review's *Cracking the ACT*.

What Is the ACT?

The ACT is a standardized exam used for college admissions. Every year, it is administered to more than one million college-bound students just like you. You can take the test in September, October, December, February (in all states except New York), April, or June. Colleges use the test to evaluate your likelihood of succeeding in college. Unfortunately, the test does a lousy job of showing how well you'll do in college. It also does not measure your intelligence. Ultimately, the only thing the ACT shows is how well you do on the ACT.

The structure of the ACT is always the same. Whether you take it in New York City in October or in St. Louis in December, you're going to see the following tests in the following order:

- a 45-minute English test with 75 questions
- a 60-minute Math test with 60 questions
- a 35-minute Reading test with 40 questions
- a 35-minute Science test with 40 questions
- an optional 30-minute Writing test with 1 essay prompt

English

The English test has five passages in it, each with fifteen questions. The passages are pretty straightforward, and the questions contain a roughly even mix of questions on grammar or punctuation and on the style and content of the passage. The subject matter for the passages is completely unpredictable, but they are often written in the first person, as though the author were telling you a story.

Math

The Math test always is made up of the following questions:

- 14 pre-algebra questions
- 10 elementary algebra questions
- 9 intermediate algebra questions
- 9 coordinate geometry questions
- 14 plane geometry questions
- 4 trigonometry questions

These questions are arranged in a rough order of difficulty. The easiest questions do not come first, and the toughest questions do not show up only at the end. Although there is a general trend of increasing difficulty throughout the Math test, there are usually some easy questions among the final ten questions and some tough questions in the first half of the section.

Reading

The Reading test is made up of four passages, each with ten questions. They appear in the following order:

- prose fiction
- social science
- humanities
- natural science

Each passage is roughly 85–90 lines long. The prose fiction passage is an excerpt from a novel or short story published relatively recently (usually something from the past twenty years, at most). The excerpts are frequently concerned with the author's ethnicity. The social science passage is usually a discussion of some aspect of our society. The humanities passage can be on just about any topic you can think of, from Japanese cabinet making to olive farming in Spain. The natural science passage is just what it sounds like, only there are usually no scientific figures accompanying the passage. There's just reading in this test.

Science

The Science test contains three types of passages:

- 3 charts and graphs passages with 5 questions each
- 3 experiments passages with 6 questions each
- 1 "fighting scientists" passage with 7 questions

The passages in this section are on a variety of topics, including biology, physics, and earth science. What is absolutely crucial to remember is that you don't need to know anything about science to be able to do well on this part of the test (more on that later). The questions on the Science test do not come in any order of difficulty. There is also no order to the passages themselves. Your ACT may start with a charts and graphs passage, or it may not. You never can tell until you open it up.

Writing

The ACT Writing test has one essay prompt, and you'll have 30 minutes to craft a response. The prompt defines an issue and presents three points of view on the issue; you will be asked to respond to a question by analyzing the three positions, coming up with your own view on the issue, and explaining how your position relates to the other three. While the topics in the past have related directly to high school life, the present topics cover a diverse range of issues. One prompt asked students to assess the growing presence of technology in our lives. Does our reliance on machines take away part of our humanity? Are automatons a good solution for tackling mindless, repetitive jobs? Do intelligent machines force us to broaden what we consider human? What is your position on the rising sub-class of increasingly intelligent robots? The strange thing about the Writing test is that it isn't a mandatory part of the ACT. When you register for the test, you'll have to decide whether you need to take this part of the exam. We'll talk more about that later.

Experimental Sections

Although the SAT routinely features an experimental section that is not counted toward your score, the ACT does not. Only in the June administration does the ACT contain an experimental section. This section will come at the end of the test (it will be section 5) and will be irregular in a couple of easy-to-spot ways. It will have an unusual number of questions. For example, if it is a Math test, instead of having 60 questions, it may have just 13. It will also last for a strange amount of time. For example, if it is an English test, it may last for 20 minutes instead of 45.

Frequently, the proctor of the exam will tell you that this section will not count toward your score. Whether or not you do well just doesn't matter. So why is it there? ACT is testing new questions on you. If you feel like helping with this, great. Go ahead and do your best on the experimental section. If you don't feel like helping ACT with its little research project, then take a nap for 20 minutes. It won't matter at all.

How Is It Scored?

After taking the ACT, you will receive a number of primary scores and a series of accompanying readiness scores and indicators. You will get a scaled score between 1 and 36 for the English, Math, Reading, and Science tests. These four scores are then averaged to create your composite score, which is also on a 1–36 scale.

If you do take the Writing test, you will receive an additional score: your Writing score, which will range from 1–36. This score is not factored into the composite, so taking the Writing test will not have a direct impact on your composite score. Be sure to check ACT's website to determine whether your target schools want you to take the ACT Writing test.

Starting in the fall of 2015, you'll also be receiving readiness scores and indicators. These include the following:

- **STEM score.** This score will show you how well you did in the Math and Science portions of the test.

- **Progress Toward Career Readiness Indicator.** The ACT would have you believe this indicator measures how prepared you are for a career, but really it just measures how prepared you are to take yet another test: the ACT National Career Readiness Certificate™.

- **English Language Arts Score.** If you take the Writing test, this score will give you a combined score for the English, Reading, and Writing section.

- **Text Complexity Progress Indicator.** This score will tell you how well you fared on those hard passages throughout the test.

Where Does the ACT Come From?

The ACT is written by a company called ACT in Iowa City, Iowa. This company writes a number of other exams, some of which you may already have taken, like the PLAN, and some of which you may take in the future, like the MCAT. ACT is not an educational institution, nor does it have education as its goal. All it does is evaluate people with its tests.

It does have relationships with colleges and universities that accept ACT scores as part of their admissions processes. All schools, by the way, that require a standardized test accept either the SAT or the ACT.

The test itself is not written by college professors. Questions are written by people from a wide variety of backgrounds, many of them high school teachers in the Iowa City area. The intent of ACT is to have its test reflect what is being taught in high schools across America, and so the content of the exam is routinely reviewed by a panel of high school–level educators. Exciting stuff, eh? You should not feel intimidated by the ACT—it is by no means a measure of your worth or ability.

How Important Is the ACT?

The ACT is just one part of your college application, and it's not necessarily the most important part. Your grades are more important than your ACT score, and your personal statement and extracurricular activities matter as well. Remember: A bad ACT score may keep you out of a school, but a good ACT score alone will never be enough to get you in. (A great ACT score is another matter. Many state schools have programs to admit students solely on the basis of their ACT scores.) Every year, many people who score 30 or higher on the ACT are rejected by great colleges because of problems with the rest of their applications. The important way in which the ACT is different from the other parts of your application is that it's the one thing you can change quickly.

When Should You Take the ACT?

You should start taking the ACT in your junior year. Because you can choose not to report your scores to colleges, taking the test several times does not hurt you. While there is a maximum number of times you can take the ACT (12), we doubt anyone would *want* to take it that many times. The best thing to do is to take the test early in your junior year and **don't** send the scores anywhere. See how you do, work on your weaknesses, take it again, and **don't** send those scores anywhere either. If you want to work on it some more, great. Just repeat the process until you're satisfied. Once you have scores that you like (or once you're sick of taking the test), notify ACT of which scores you want to send to colleges.

ACT Score Choice—Controlling Information

ACT allows you to control who sees your scores. If you leave the high school code blank (Box L on the registration form) and leave the college and scholarship code section blank (Box O on the registration form) when you sign up for the test, ACT will send your scores to you and no one else. Later, when you tell ACT to send scores to colleges, it sends only the scores you specify. This way, no matter how many times you take the ACT, all colleges ever see is the one score you want them to see. They don't know how many times you took the test and they can't find out. (One important note: If you are using ACT scores to establish academic eligibility to play sports at a Division I or II school, you may need to report scores from more than one ACT administration. Discuss this with your coach or counselor.)

There are also some schools that require you to list all of your test scores. In other words, they do not want you to select only the ones you want. Research your schools carefully to find out if any on your list fall into this category and abide by the school's recommendations and requirements.

There are other reasons you may wish to release several scores. Many schools "super score," which means they calculate a composite based on your best English, best Math, best Reading, and best Science from all of your administrations. The Common Application similarly asks you to list the same. If all this is confusing, here's a simple pair of scenarios. If you take the ACT 3 times and score a 25, 25, and a 27, send only the 27. But if you take it 3 times and score 25 each time, with one subject going up only as another falls, send all 3 on the chance that school super scores. Or heed the advice we mentioned in last paragraph: Research your schools carefully.

May I See My ACT, Please?

In December, April, and June, ACT allows you to order a copy of the ACT you take (it is not sent out until after the test, of course). Along with the test book, you get the answers you gave to each question. This is an invaluable tool for you if you intend to retake the test, as it allows you to see exactly where you need to focus your efforts. If it's at all possible, sign up for one of those three test dates and order your test booklet. It costs extra, but it's worthwhile.

Sign Me Up

You can register for the ACT several ways. How you register might depend on whether you have any special circumstances. If you are planning to take the ACT on one of the nationally administered dates, or if you are retaking the exam, you can simply sign up online at www.act.org or use ACT's paper registration packet. Although online registration is probably easiest, there are a number of situations that require you to use the registration packet. You must use the registration packet if you

- need disability accommodations
- need to change your test center or test date
- are testing outside the United States
- are using a state-funded voucher or fee waiver
- are enrolled in grade 6, 7, 8, or 9
- do not have a Visa or MasterCard

If you've registered for a national test date within the last two years, you can also register via telephone.

Be sure to register for your test date at least 4–5 weeks before the actual exam; if you don't, you will have to pay an additional late registration fee. You will also incur additional fees if you do any of the following:

- send your scores to more than four colleges or universities
- take the ACT Writing test
- change your test date or test center
- test standby
- register by telephone (for repeat test takers)
- test outside the United States
- choose to view your score early
- order the Test Information Release (selected dates only)

As you can see, there are a number of fun ways to increase the cost of your ACT experience. Be sure to refer to ACT's student website (www. actstudent.org) for the most recent pricing information.

How Should I Use
Crash Course for the ACT?

This book will provide you with great techniques for raising your ACT score, but you should supplement it with practice. Our book *1,460 ACT Practice Questions* will give you plenty of just that—1,460 questions to be exact—in English, Math, Reading, Science, and Writing.

You can also download an ACT from ACT's web site, www.act.org. It's the same test that is printed in the registration booklet, which your guidance counselor office may have. This may be easier than killing your printer.

Read *Crash Course for the ACT* and work the drills, and then practice what you've learned on the tests. If you're not happy with your performance, rework the material in the book, review the questions you missed on your practice test, and then take another practice test. Don't try to do all of this in one day; take a look at how much time you have before the ACT and spread the work out over that period.

General
Strategy

Be Test-Wise

The better you know the ACT, the better you are going to perform. Although our Ten Steps will discuss approaches to each of the four sections of the ACT, there are some general principles that we need to discuss before you go any further. You can use these techniques throughout the entire test, so give this chapter a good, careful read before moving on to the Ten Steps.

You Paid for It—You Should Write on It

One of the biggest mistakes people make when taking the ACT is that they do the work in their heads. Whenever you are working on the ACT—whether it's preparing with this book, taking a practice test, or taking the real thing—you should be writing everything down on the page. Keep nothing in your head. The ACT is a well-designed test, and one of the things it is designed to do is take advantage of your inclinations. Most people prefer to work through problems as quickly as they can, and writing stuff down just slows them down, so they don't do it. This is a bad approach to take with the ACT.

The questions on the ACT are full of partial answers, misleading answers, and distracting answers that are there to trip you up. If you're doing work in your head (and this goes for the Reading, English, and Science tests, too, not just Math), you're going to fall into one of their traps. So, anytime you complete a step to a problem, write it down. Anytime you need to do a calculation, write it down. Anytime you note something important in a Reading passage, write down where it is. Anytime you find a value you need in a table on the Science test, circle it. Never keep track of this stuff in your head.

On the Math test you will use your calculator a lot, and the temptation is to just plug everything into it and see what answers you get but never write anything on your test booklet. Bad idea. There's no need to work out the math on paper (that's what the calculator is for, after all), but you must set the problems up on paper or risk making careless errors that will cost you points. The folks who write the math questions write the question first, the right answer second, and the wrong answers last. The wrong answers aren't randomly selected; they are the answers that come up if you make simple mistakes when calculating—exactly the kinds of mistakes you make when you don't keep track of your work on paper. So keep that pencil moving and write all over the test.

Work Is Work and Bubbling Is Bubbling

Spend your time wisely on the ACT. When you are doing problems, let that be your focus. You don't want go back and forth between the test booklet and your answer sheet to bubble your answers. You should focus on a group of problems, and you've finished them, you should then bubble in the answers for all of them. Going back and forth hurts your focus.

On the English test, complete an entire passage of 15 questions before bubbling in the answers for any of them. On the Math test, do a page of problems and then bubble all the answers from that page. On the Reading test, do all of the questions for a single passage and then bubble those 10 answers. On the Science test, do a full passage (5 to 7 questions, depending on what type of passage it is) and then bubble in the answers for that passage. If you're always shifting between problem solving and bubbling, you're not spending your energy wisely.

Never Ever Leave a Bubble Empty

The ACT does not have a guessing penalty (though its cousin, the SAT, does). That means if you leave a question blank or get it wrong, the effect on your score is the same—nothing is subtracted. So, even if you can't answer a question, never leave it blank because there's a chance that even if you just guess blindly, you'll get it right.

The computers scoring your test don't know if you're guessing and treat correct guesses the way they do any other correct answers—by giving you points for them. So, when you have two minutes left in a test, stop what you're doing and put answers down for all the questions you haven't answered (leave the one you're working on and three or four more blank in case you have time to work on them after filling in all of the other bubbles). Don't spend time trying to figure out what letter is more likely to come up or what answer you've already used a lot in this section. There's no one answer choice that comes up most frequently, so just bubble in the same answer for everything. It all evens out in the end.

Process of Elimination

Process of Elimination (POE) is a great tool on the ACT. Here's how it works and why it can be so useful. Every question has one right answer and three (or four, if it's a math question) wrong answers. Your goal, of course, is to find the right answer, but how you reach that goal is irrelevant. If you work a problem out the "right" way, guess blindly, or play "eeny, meeny, miny, moe" with the answer choices, you will score points as long as you choose the correct one. The problem is that finding the right answer can be pretty tricky sometimes. That's where POE comes in.

If you can identify all of the wrong answers in a question, you've also found the right answer, because it's the only one left, and that's great. If you can identify a couple of wrong answers in a question, that's still great, because if you have to guess, you've made it more likely that you're going to guess right.

For every question, pay attention to the answer choices. You'll find that you can eliminate obvious wrong answers in every section of the test, especially in the Math test. Every time you figure out that a certain answer choice is wrong, be sure to cross it out so that you don't accidentally pick it. POE is so powerful on the Math test that we've given it its own chapter and renamed it Ballparking for that section. Don't forget to use POE on the other sections, too. There are crazy wrong answers on every section—eliminating them is easy and will raise your score.

Use Your Time Wisely

The ACT is an important part of college admissions (though it's not the most important part, as we discussed in the previous chapter), and clearly, you take it seriously or you wouldn't have bought this book. So when you take the test, you need to be mentally and physically ready, and you can't afford to zone out at any time during the exam.

When you take the ACT, use every minute they give you to work the questions. If you finish a test early and spend the remaining time staring out the window, taking a little nap, or thinking about the best place to go for lunch after the ACT, you are lowering your score. If you get through all 60 math questions in less than 60 minutes, go back and check your work. If you're like most people, there might be problems you'll give up on because they take too much time. This is the time to go back to those problems and work on them some more (you sure can't do that when time is up). If you finish the Science or Reading tests early, go back to problems you gave up on—the answer is always right there on the page in those sections, and the only way you'll find it is by spending more time looking for it. Sure, it's a drag, but it's also the only way to get the best score you can (you do want a good score, don't you?). And besides, you paid to be there, right? So make the most of your time.

Maintain Your Brain

One problem a lot of people have on the ACT is having enough energy to finish. Four hours is a long time to be sitting still and taking a test, and because it's sandwiched between breakfast and lunch, you're probably going to be hungry by the end of it. So eat a good breakfast the day of the test and bring a snack for the break.

While the other kids are talking during the break about that awful geometry question, go somewhere quiet, eat your snack, and keep your cool. They don't know anything about the exam that could possibly help you on the rest of it, and they may actually succeed in making you more nervous than you already are, so hang out on your own and keep focused. There are just two tests after the break (or three, if you take the Writing test) and they're both short, but they count as much as the first two, so they can make or break your score.

Be Prepared

If you're taking the ACT at an unfamiliar location, drive there the night before so that you're sure where you're going on test day. This is especially wise if you are taking the exam on a college campus. College campuses tend to be large and have very few maps. You can bet that most of the college students aren't going to be wandering around campus early on a Saturday, either, so you'll have no one to help you if you don't know where you're going. This is a good time to make sure the car has gas in it, too.

Oh yeah, this probably goes without saying, but don't go out the night before the ACT. Stay home, watch a movie, and go to bed at a reasonable hour. Definitely don't stay out with your friends until two o'clock in the morning and expect to do a good job the next day. Before you go to bed, get your stuff ready for the exam; scrambling around looking for your registration ticket the morning of the ACT really isn't good for your nerves.

On the day of the exam be sure to dress in layers. The heating and cooling systems of schools can be very unpredictable, as you know. Even if you're taking the ACT in your own school, remember that you could wind up in any room in the school, so you're better off with a flexible wardrobe. You want to be able to throw something on if you're too cold or take something off if you're too warm, so dress accordingly.

Leave your house in plenty of time. Although the directions on your admission ticket instruct you to show up at 8:00 A.M., don't cut it that short. Late arrivals are NOT admitted to the ACT, so get there no later than 7:45 A.M. You want a stress-free morning before the exam begins.

What You Need for the ACT

Get all this stuff ready the night before the exam. You don't want to be running around looking for a calculator, trying to eat breakfast, and getting yelled at for not being ready on the morning of your big test, do you? Of course not. So use this handy checklist to guarantee a streamlined morning:

☐ Admission ticket (or completed registration bulletin and check if you're going to register on the spot)

☐ Sharpened No. 2 pencils (bring at least 3 or 4, but leave the mechanical pencils at home. You can't use them on the ACT.)

☐ Calculator (bring the one you use every day at school, and put fresh batteries in it, too)

☐ Backup calculator (hey, calculators break, too)

☐ Quiet watch, so you can keep track of time in case the proctor doesn't

☐ Snack (some fruit, some candy, maybe even a box of juice)

☐ Photo ID (required!)

PART II

Ten Steps to the ACT

Step 1:
If It Ain't Broke, Don't Fix It

What Is In the English Test?

On the English test of the ACT, you'll be given a passage with some portions underlined. Your job is to look at the underlined phrase and decide whether it's correct. If it's not, you'll have to fix it. Remember that 25 percent of the underlined words or phrases are perfect just the way they are. Don't make the mistake of finding problems where they don't exist.

There are two types of questions on the English test: questions about grammar or punctuation and questions about the structure and style of the passage. This chapter is concerned with grammar and punctuation. We'll talk about structure and style in the next chapter.

The Big Technique: If It Ain't Broke, Don't Fix It

Anything that is not underlined in the English test is perfect just the way it is. Use those sentences to guide you in evaluating the underlined portions. Frequently, the underlined part depends on the non-underlined part. If you keep in mind that both parts have to agree, you'll do much better on this section.

Because pretty much every question is going to hinge on its relationship to the parts of the passage that aren't underlined, you've got to read the entire passage as you go, and pay close attention to it as you do so. You can't skip from question to question on this test.

No Change

On the grammar and punctuation questions you'll always have the option of leaving the underlined stuff alone. The first answer choice on these questions is always *NO CHANGE*. Don't be afraid to choose this. As we mentioned above, it's right 25 percent of the time. When you come to an underlined word or phrase, your natural response is to assume that there must be something wrong with it. There might not be. Be sure to find a mistake before you decide to fix it.

Use the Answer Choices

When you're doing the English test, pay attention to what is going on in the answer choices—it will help you do the questions. If your answer choices offer different forms of the same verb, you know that you need to determine what tense should be used. If your answer choices position commas in different places, you know that you need to make a decision about comma placement. If your answer choices offer you periods, commas, and no punctuation, you know that you have to decide whether to break up the sentences. The point is, the answers will tell you what to focus on when doing the question. If all the answers have the same form of the verb, you know that you don't need to worry about that and you can focus your energy on the real problem.

Stop! Go!

On the English test, you'll be tested on your ability to properly place punctuation. What the writers of the test want to know is if you know when to use a period, when to use a comma, and when to use nothing at all. That's where stop/go comes in.

If you are offered a choice that involves commas and periods, you know that you need to decide whether to start a new sentence. The only time you want to end one sentence and start another is when each of the two sentences you're going to create is a complete idea. Two complete ideas mean stop. If either one is an incomplete idea, you'll have to go.

Stop Punctuation	Go Punctuation
.	,
!	:
?	—
;	and
, and	but
, but	(no punctuation)

Complete Ideas and Incomplete Ideas

A complete idea is something that can stand on its own. It has a subject and a verb, and it doesn't have anything in it that needs to be continued. Here are some complete ideas:

> I worked out today.

> The sun never came out, but that didn't stop people from going to the beach.

> It was possible to hear the television after the hammering stopped, but it didn't matter because the commercial was already over.

An incomplete idea might have a subject and a verb or it might not. Incomplete ideas can never stand on their own, however. Here are some incomplete ideas, along with explanations of why they're incomplete.

> Developed further into a serious problem for the team.

We don't know what it is that developed—there's no subject here.

> After she picked up the groceries, which were heavier than she had expected, and went back to the mall.

The word "After" at the beginning is never resolved. "After" she did all that stuff . . . what happened? We're never told, so this is incomplete.

The Breath Test

When you're doing a stop/go question, read the non-underlined part of the sentence both before and after the place where ACT offers you the stop punctuation. If both parts are complete ideas, choose stop punctuation. If either part is an incomplete idea, you must choose go punctuation. If you have a choice between a comma and no punctuation, use the breath test. Read the sentence in your head, and if you feel like you would need to pause for a breath when reading it aloud, you need a comma.

Let's try some stop/go questions from part of a typical ACT passage:

On December 21, 1937, Walt Disney's first feature-length animated film, *Snow White and the Seven Dwarfs*, premiered in Hollywood. Although we think of this film as a <u>classic. When it was released, it</u>
₁
represented an enormous departure from the prevailing standards for animation.

Although *Snow White* was not the first animated feature (a distinction held by an Argentinean film, *The Apostle*), it is easily one of the most significant animated films ever made. Prior to *Snow White*, most animation was in the form of short, silly <u>films that</u> were presented prior to a live-
₂
action feature film. These shorts, though often colorful, inventive, and hilarious, were not considered to be serious fare. They were filler that took up time before the films people really wanted to see.

1. **A.** NO CHANGE
   B. classic; it was released and
   C. classic, when it was released it
   D. classic when it was released it

2. **F.** NO CHANGE
   G. films—that
   H. films—which
   J. films. That

The first thing you want to do on the questions is look at the answer choices. Because the answers for question number 1 offer us a semicolon, a comma, and a period (in the passage originally), we can be pretty sure that this is a stop/go question. So, look at what comes before and after where the period is and decide if you want to stop or go.

Before the period we have "Although we think of this film as a classic." That's not a complete idea. The word "Although" sets up some sort of contrast, but the second half of the contrast would be missing if we used a period here. Whenever we have an incomplete idea we have to use go punctuation. So, cross out all the stop punctuation (A and B).

Now it's a question of comma or no comma. Use the breath test. Do you want to pause between "classic" and "when" as you read this sentence to yourself? If you said yes, you're right. The answer is C.

Looking at question number 2, we see that the answer choices again present both stop and go punctuation, so let's take a look at what comes before the underlined words: "Prior to *Snow White*, most animation was in the form of short, silly films." Can the sentence stand on its own? Yep. It's a complete idea. Now we have to look at what comes after the underlined part and make sure it's a complete idea as well: "that were presented prior to a live-action feature film." Hmm. This isn't a complete idea. Because we have a complete idea followed by an incomplete idea, we're going to have to use go punctuation. The question is, which kind? We've got both dashes and no punctuation to consider.

Use the breath test again. Would you pause between "films" and "that" when you read this aloud? Nope. So the answer is F.

Commas, Commas, Commas

The test writers at ACT love to test commas on the English test. One way they'll test commas is as go punctuation, as we've just seen. Another way is by using them to set off unnecessary parts of a sentence. How will you know you're looking at a comma question? The answers will contain mostly commas (and maybe a dash).

Commas in this situation will come in pairs—one before the unnecessary phrase and one after. The way to tell if they are placed properly is to read the sentence and leave out the stuff between the commas. If it sounds okay that way, then the commas are correct. If it doesn't, then they're not. Take a look at these examples:

> The weather that day was, unfortunately,
>
> not very good.

This is a proper use of commas. You could remove the word "unfortunately" and this sentence would be fine.

> They drove off in their car, after having a
>
> couple of tacos, and sodas.

This is wrong. If you lifted out "after having a couple of tacos," this sentence would be nonsense.

Try these comma questions from the same passage you saw earlier:

> In the early days of American animation,
>
> most shorts were produced in New York
>
> City. From the Fleischer brothers' studio
>
> came *Betty Boop*, Sullivan Studio produced
>
> *Felix the Cat*, and Aesop Fables Studio
>
> produced a series of shorts featuring the
> [3]

farmer Al Falfa. These studios churned out shorts at an astonishing pace that some-times reached one <u>new, though low-quality</u>
₄
short per week.

> 3. **A.** NO CHANGE
> **B.** *Boop*; Sullivan Studio produced *Felix the Cat*,
> **C.** *Boop*, Sullivan Studio produced *Felix the Cat*
> **D.** *Boop*—Sullivan Studio produced *Felix the Cat*,

> 4. **F.** NO CHANGE
> **G.** new, low-quality,
> **H.** new, though, low-quality
> **J.** new, though low-quality,

In question number 3 we've got items in a list. ACT always wants you to put a comma before the "and" in a list, so eliminate C right away. You don't want to mix and match semicolons and commas, so B is out, and the same thing goes for commas and dashes, so get rid of D. The answer is A—this one is fine as written.

In question number 4 the answers have commas scattered all over the place, so we need to figure out where they should go. Does the sentence work as written? No—the word "though" is awkward this way, and that comma right after "new" doesn't work. Something's off here, so eliminate F. Be sure to cross it out so that you don't pick it accidentally. Answer G changes the meaning of the sentence by dropping "though," and you're never allowed to change the meaning, so ditch it. Now it's down to H or J. Try eliminating the words between the commas for both. When you do that for H you get "one new low-quality short," which isn't the meaning they had, so dump it. With J you get "one new short," which sounds fine. Choice J is the best answer.

Don't Be Tense—Just Use the Right Verb

The key to getting verb questions right on the ACT is to match the underlined verb with the verbs in the rest of the passage. Figure out what is going on in the non-underlined part and you'll be able to get the right verb in the underlined part every time. Avoid the passive voice whenever you can.

Walt Disney defied all of the prevailing animation trends in making *Snow White*. It was long, the story was far from comical, and he spent three years (and $1.4 million) making it. The demands of *Snow White* nearly bankrupted his company, but, in the end, the breakthrough *Snow White* represented was clearly worth the cost. *Snow White* establishes the animated feature as a new genre of American film and brought animation to heights it hadn't experienced since Winsor McCay's *Gertie the Dinosaur*. *Snow White*, in presenting fully developed animated characters that audiences cared about. It is said that at the premiere, John Barrymore was moved to tears.

5. **A.** NO CHANGE
   B. *Snow White* established the animated feature
   C. *Snow White* made the animated feature
   D. *Snow White* established the animated feature,

6. **F.** NO CHANGE
   G. *Snow White* presents fully developed animation
   H. *Snow White*'s present fully develops animated
   J. *Snow White* presented fully developed animated

In question number 5, three of the four answer choices do something with the verb, so let's start there. What tense is being used in the rest of the passage? We have "defied," "spent," "bankrupted," and "represented" before this point, and the later verbs are also in the past tense, so "establishes" must be wrong. Eliminate A. Now, B and C are essentially the same. What happens with "made" being substituted for "established"? It doesn't work because of the "as" in the non-underlined part. You can't say "made . . . as," and because you can't change the "as," we have to eliminate C. So do we want the comma or not? Use the breath test and you'll see that there's no need to pause after "feature," so eliminate D. Choice B is the correct answer.

In question number 6, the verbs are being changed in all the answer choices, so this is another verb question. We already figured out in the last problem that we want the past tense, so G and H are out (H also changed the subject from *Snow White* to Snow White's present—ACT will often put more than one mistake into wrong answers). Choice F would work as past tense, but not in this sentence because it creates an incomplete idea: "Snow White, in presenting fully developed animated characters . . . "—then what? What happened next? Because it's an incomplete idea, it's out, so the correct answer is J.

Contraction Expansion

Another small item that counts for a lot on the ACT is the apostrophe. The apostrophe is used for two major things that are tested: contraction and possession.

When used to indicate a contraction, the apostrophe is generally marking where letters are missing from the contracted words. For example, when "do not" is written as "don't," the apostrophe marks the missing "o." Similarly, when "should have" is written as "should've," the apostrophe marks the missing "h" and "a."

Although you may have had English teachers tell you that good writing doesn't use contractions, the folks who write the ACT English test disagree. As far as they're concerned, good writing *definitely* uses contractions.

It's rare to see a question with an improperly constructed contraction (like, say, "cann't" for "can't"). In fact, there's only one contraction ACT tests regularly (we'll discuss it just before the drill at the end of this section). What are typically tested are homonyms—words that sound the same but have different spellings and different meanings. So you'll have to choose between answers such as "there" and "they're" and "their." What ACT is counting on is that you will just "listen" to the answers in your head and not think about what *meaning* is called for. But you know better than that, don't you?

When used to indicate possession, there are a couple of ways to throw in the apostrophe, both of which involve the letter "s." The simplest way to explain is via example: A book owned by a dog is *the dog's book*; a goofball in your math class might be *the class's clown*. You may be wondering if they'll give you a choice between something like "the boss's daughter," "the boss' daughter," and "the bosss' daughter." They do NOT test this. Rest easy.

What they DO test is the difference between *its*, *it's*, and *its'*. This comes up on almost every test, so learn it now and guarantee yourself some points.

Term	Meaning
IT'S	This is the contraction of "it is" or "it has." It never has any other meanings. If you can't replace "it's" with "it is" or "it has" and maintain the meaning of the sentence, pick something else. You'll probably want "its."
ITS	This is the possessive form of the pronoun "it." Here's an example that uses "its" correctly: "I liked the movie, especially its ending."
ITS'	This is not a word under *any* circumstances (well, not in English, anyway). Do not pick it, EVER! Honest!!

<u>Its</u> been said that there is no task more
1
difficult than raising children. Relative
to other mammals, human children spend
an extremely long time with their parents
before setting out on their own. Although
hundreds of years ago children may have
been expected to work, marry, and start
families of their own as early as 13 or 14
years of age, it is currently not uncommon
to find children living in <u>their</u> <u>parents home</u>
2   3
well into their twenties.

1. **A.** NO CHANGE
   B. It's
   C. Its'
   D. It is

2. **F.** NO CHANGE
   G. there
   H. they're
   J. his

3. **A.** NO CHANGE
   B. parent's home
   C. parents' home
   D. home of their parents

In question number 1 they want to see if you know the right form. Well, what is happening at the beginning of the sentence? It's a contraction of "It has," so you need the properly contracted form. Choice D is no good because "is" is the wrong tense. Choice C isn't a word. And A is possessive, so B is the right answer.

In question number 2 they're seeing if you know which of these sound-alike forms is the right one. First, look at J. Could "his" work? No, because children is plural. You want the pronoun here, and you want it to be possessive, so F is the right answer. Choice G just sounds the same, but deals with locations, not people, and H introduces an extra verb and causes other problems as well.

In question number 3 you need to know the right way to make a possessive. Choice D is out because you'd be repeating "their." Choice A is out because you need an apostrophe. So is it B or C? Well, both are grammatically correct, but one is for a single "parent" and the other for a pair of "parents." Earlier in the paragraph it was made clear that we're talking about both "parents," so C is correct.

I Agree

Subjects and verbs have to agree in sentences. If you have a plural subject, you need a plural verb. Similarly, pronouns must agree with the nouns they replace. "Jim" needs to be replaced with "he," not "it" or "she." As obvious as all of this sounds, it is still tested on every single ACT, so you need to watch for it. How will you recognize these sorts of questions? By the answer choices, of course. If you see verbs in both plural and singular form or a bunch of different pronouns, you can be sure that agreement is one of the things ACT is testing in the question. To do these sorts of questions, match the underlined text with the non-underlined portion of the passage, as usual.

Animated <u>film is</u> now an accepted part of
the film world, with several released in this
country every year. Although they don't
all ~~rise to the~~ level of *Snow White*, many
excellent features continue to be produced,
including films such as Tim Burton's
Nightmare Before Christmas and 1999's
excellent *The Iron Giant*. Like *Snow White*
before them, these films give the audience
characters <u>they can care</u> about along with
superior animation.

7. **A.** NO CHANGE
   B. films are
   C. films' are
   D. film's is

8. **F.** NO CHANGE
   G. you can care
   H. it can care
   J. who can care

In question number 7 there are two answers with "is" and two
with "are." The thing to do, then, is decide whether the subject is
singular or plural. The answer choices offer both options, so we'll
have to go to the non-underlined part (again!). In the first part of
the sentence, it seems that either would work, but in the second
part, the word "several" forces you to select a plural subject, so
eliminate A and D. Now, is there any need for that apostrophe? No,
nothing is being possessed by the films, so dump C. The answer is
B.

In question number 8 we're dealing with pronouns. In pronoun
questions first determine what the pronoun refers to. The verb
connected to the pronoun "they" is "care," so answer the question
"Who can care?" and you'll have the subject. The subject here is
"audience," so the pronoun is supposed to refer to the audience.

"Audience" is singular, so F is out, because "they" is plural. Choice J makes "characters" the subject, so it's out, too. "You" aren't the audience, so that takes care of G. The answer is H. By the way, even though the audience is composed of many people, it is actually an "it," not a "they."

Step 2: Make the Transition

The English test will always include questions that deal with the flow of the passage. These questions can focus on linking sentences, connecting paragraphs, or just about anything else related to the logical flow of the passage. These questions will sometimes look like grammar questions, but their content will be different. One type of question in this family is the transition question.

The Big Technique: Make the Transition

Transition questions focus on transition words—*yet, however, therefore*—words that link two ideas and emphasize how they are different or how they are similar. Your job on this type of question is to look at the non-underlined parts before and after the question and decide how they are connected. Does one explain the other? Does the second one contradict the first? Do they provide two similar thoughts on the same topic? These are the questions to ask yourself on a transition question.

There are many words that can be used as transition words. Here are some transition words that ACT likes to test:

Transition Words	
Similar	**Different**
and	however
thus	yet
therefore	although
since	still

Let's try some transition questions from the passage on animation we saw in the last chapter.

On December 21, 1937, Walt Disney's first feature-length animated film, *Snow White and the Seven Dwarfs*, premiered in Hollywood. Although we think of this film as a classic, when it was released, it represented an enormous departure from the prevailing standards for animation.

Because[1] *Snow White* was not the first animated feature (a distinction held by an Argentinean film, *The Apostle*), it is easily one of the most significant animated films ever made. Prior to[2] *Snow White*, most animation was in the form of short, silly films that were presented prior to a live-action feature film. These shorts, though often colorful, inventive, and hilarious, were not considered to be serious fare. They were filler that took up time before the films people really wanted to see.

1. **A.** NO CHANGE
   B. Although
   C. In fact,
   D. However,

2. **F.** NO CHANGE
   G. Like
   H. Because of
   J. OMIT the underlined portion

In question number 1 we've got a classic ACT transition question. You have to decide among *Because*, *Although*, *In fact*, and *However*. So you need to decide what sort of transition is called for here. Read the non-underlined part. The first half of the sentence tells you what

Snow White was not (the first animated feature); the second half tells you what it was (significant). Those are contrasting ideas, so you need a contrasting transition word. Eliminate A and C. Choices B and D are both contrasting transition words. Which fits better? Well, *However* would work nicely if it were between the two ideas, but it's not. The contrasting ideas both come after this point in the sentence, so that leaves us with *Although*. Choice B is the correct answer.

In question number 2 we have a different sort of transition—it's one of logical flow in the meaning of the passage. To make things interesting, they've even thrown *OMIT* in as an option. Although *OMIT* is correct more than 25 percent of the time, it's not what we need here—if the sentence began "*Snow White*, most animation . . ." it wouldn't make any sense at all, so eliminate J (be sure to physically cross it out). If we picked G, the passage would make the claim that *Snow White* was also a short, silly film, and we know that's not true (it's stated in the passage later, and we already know it's a feature film, not a short), so G is out. Choice H is ridiculous; there's no way that one film could be responsible for all other films being short and silly. Dump H. The correct answer is F.

NOTE: OMIT is one of four answer choices, but it's correct **far** more than 25 percent of the time. When it's an option, assume it's right until you find a truly better choice.

Words These Order in Put the Right

Another type of style and structure question you'll see will be the scrambled word question. Now, while they won't do anything as ridiculous as what we just did in the heading for this section, they will present you with some fairly screwed-up options. The reason these questions are tricky is that the underlined portion is long, and so is each of the answer choices. You sometimes have to spend a lot of time picking through each choice in order to get to the right one. Be sure to aggressively cross out the ones you eliminate as you go or you're liable to waste a lot of time rereading answer choices.

The key to doing well on this type of question is slowing down and focusing on the logic of the sentence. The wrong answers will put commas in strange places or have events happen in the wrong order (for example, an egg will hatch before it is laid).

Try some more questions from our animation passage:

In the early days of American animation, most shorts were produced in New York City. From the Fleischer brothers' studio came *Betty Boop*, Sullivan Studio produced *Felix the Cat*, and Aesop Fables Studio produced a series of shorts featuring the farmer Al Falfa. These studios churned out shorts at an astonishing pace that sometimes reached <u>one new short each low-quality week.</u> Walt Disney <u>defied all of the prevailing anima-</u>[3] <u>tion trends in making *Snow White*</u>[4]. It was long, the story was far from comical, and he[4] spent three years (and $1.4 million) making it. The demands of *Snow White* nearly bankrupted his company, but, in the end, the breakthrough *Snow White* represented was clearly worth the cost. *Snow White* established the animated feature as a new genre of American film and brought animation to heights it hadn't experienced since Winsor McCay's *Gertie the Dinosaur. Snow White* presented fully developed animated characters that audiences cared about. It is said that at the premiere, John Barrymore was moved to tears.

Animated films are <u>now an accepted part</u>
₅
<u>of today's film world,</u> with several released
₅
in this country every year. Although they
don't all rise to the level of *Snow White*,
many excellent features continue to be
produced, including films such as Tim
Burton's *The Nightmare Before Christmas*
and 1999's excellent *The Iron Giant*. Like
Snow White before them, these films give
the audience characters it can care about
along with superior animation.

3. **A.** NO CHANGE
   B. one new week for each low-quality short.
   C. once a week for the production of what
   could only be termed low-quality short
   animated films.
   D. one new, though low-quality, short per week.

4. **F.** NO CHANGE
   G. was the father of the animation trends defied by *Snow White*.
   H. defied Snow White in following the prevailing animation trends.
   J. defied all of the prevailing animation
   trends in making *Snow White* (the story of
   a beautiful girl banished to the woods by
   an evil queen who is jealous of her purity
   and beauty and wants to see her dead).

5. **A.** NO CHANGE
   B. accepted today as part of the film world
   C. now an accepted part of the film world,
   D. now, partly acceptable in the film world,

In question number 3 the passage as it stands doesn't make sense. The work you do in a week may be of low-quality, but the week itself cannot be. A week is just a week. Eliminate A. Choice B has the right sort of ideas, but what is a "new week"? Eliminate it. Choice C is grammatically correct and has the right meaning. It's awfully wordy, though, which is usually wrong on the ACT. If D is shorter and grammatically correct, pick it instead of C. As you can see, D does, in fact, put the adjectives where they belong and states its point more concisely than does C. Always choose the shortest grammatically correct answer. The correct answer is D.

In question number 4, G is illogical—Disney made *Snow White*, so how could he have defied himself in making it? Choice H is silly (which often happens in wrong answers on the ACT)—Snow White is just a cartoon character. So it's either J or F. These two are identical except for the explanation of the story of *Snow White* that J provides. Is it needed here? Does it fit in the rest of the paragraph? No. The paragraph is about the making of *Snow White;* this explanation, though perhaps interesting, is unnecessary. Choice F is the correct answer.

In question number 5 the passage sounds okay, but there's a small problem hiding there. By saying "now an accepted part of today's film world," a redundancy has been created. "Now" and "today" mean the same thing, so one of them must go. Cross out A. Choice B almost gets the job done, but the comma is missing. Watch out for this type of wrong answer on the test. Commas are little and easy to overlook. Cross off B. Choice D changes the meaning a bit and has an extra comma that messes everything up, so it's gone, too. The correct answer choice is C.

Did We Do It Right?

The most obvious types of style and structure questions are the ones that come at the end of the English test. They are the questions in which ACT asks if the passage answers a certain question, if the paragraphs are in the right order, or how a particular paragraph functions in the passage. You'll also sometimes see questions that ask what you would add to the passage if you wanted to make it more serious, funny, critical, or whatever.

When doing these sorts of questions, read them carefully. You must answer the exact question that's being asked, and frequently the question itself will help you to eliminate wrong answers. There's a reason that these questions are at the end of the passage—they refer to the passage as a whole. This is yet another reason that, when taking the English test, you must pay attention to the non-underlined portions.

Try some of these questions now.

On December 21, 1937, Walt Disney's first feature-length animated film, *Snow White and the Seven Dwarfs*, premiered in Hollywood. Although we think of this film as <u>classic. When it was released, represented</u>[1] an enormous departure from the prevailing standards for animation.

Although *Snow White* was not the first animated feature (a distinction held by an Argentinean film, *The Apostle*), it is easily one of the most significant animated films ever made. Prior to *Snow White*, most animation was in the form of short, silly <u>films that</u>[2] were presented prior to a live-action feature film. These shorts, though often colorful, inventive, and hilarious, were not considered to be serious fare. They were filler that took up time before the films people really wanted to see.

In the early days of American animation, most shorts were produced in New York City. From the Fleischer brothers' studio came *Betty Boop*, Sullivan Studio produced *Felix the Cat*, and Aesop Fables Studio produced a series of shorts featuring the farmer Al Falfa. These studios churned out shorts at an astonishing pace that sometimes reached one new short each low-quality week. Walt Disney defied all of the prevailing animation trends in making *Snow White*. It was long, the story was far from comical, and he spent three years (and $1.4 million) making it. The demands of *Snow White* nearly bankrupted his company, but, in the end, the breakthrough *Snow White* represented was clearly worth the cost. *Snow White* established the animated feature as a new genre of American film and brought animation to heights it hadn't experienced since Winsor McCay's *Gertie the Dinosaur*. *Snow White* presented fully developed animated characters that audiences cared about. It is said that at the premiere, John Barrymore was moved to tears.

Animated films are <u>now an accepted part</u>
<u>of today's film world</u>, with several released
^{5}
in this country every year. Although they
don't all rise to the level of *Snow White*,
many excellent features continue to be
produced, including films such as Tim
Burton's *The Nightmare Before Christmas*
and 1999's excellent *The Iron Giant*. Like
Snow White before them, these films give
the audience characters it can care about
along with superior animation.

6. Suppose a magazine editor had asked the author
to do a piece on the influence of animation on
American society. Does this essay accomplish
that goal?

  F. Yes, because it goes into detail about how
  animation in America has changed from
  something that was considered inconse-
  quential into something that touches the
  heart.

  G. Yes, because it explains how American
  society responded to *Snow White*.

  H. No, because Walt Disney's film was made
  a long time ago, and older things do not
  have an effect on modern society.

  J. No, because it doesn't discuss how American society responded to *Snow White;* it
  discusses only how *Snow White* created
  the genre of animated feature films in
  America.

7. The third paragraph of this piece, which describes some of the New York studios, serves what purpose in this essay?

    A. It provides an explanation of what American animation was like before *Snow White*.

    B. It illustrates the high quality of American animation in general.

    C. It sets up the inventiveness of the New York studios as a contrast to the work of Walt Disney in California.

    D. It summarizes the main points of the essay.

8. The author is considering adding a sentence at the end of the fourth paragraph to illustrate further the emotional connection audiences had with *Snow White* when it was released. Which of the following would best accomplish that goal?

    F. In little over three months, the film earned more than $8 million, easily making back its production cost.

    G. Even today many people enjoy showing *Snow White* to their children for the first time.

    H. Many newspaper articles of the day quote people who had just seen the film as saying that it "touched their hearts as no other feature had ever done."

    J. Barrymore was later to star in a live-action version of *Snow White*, which was also greatly successful.

There are two parts to question number 6. First, you have to answer the question "Does this essay accomplish that goal?" Then, you have to decide what the reason is. Well, does the essay discuss the influence of animation in American society? No, definitely not. It's more of a discussion of what *Snow White* was to American animation, not what animation was to society. Eliminate F and G. Now we have to decide between H and J. The best way to do that is to read the two answers and see which makes sense. Choice H says that old things have no effect on modern society. That's ridiculous! The answer must be J. When we read it, we see that it says much the same thing as we were saying earlier—*Snow White* is important to American animation.

In question number 7 you have to determine how a paragraph is used in the essay. Never do this type of question from memory. Go back, reread the paragraph, and then deal with the question. Usually, the best way to do that is by using POE. Let's take the answers one at a time. Choice A sounds pretty good. The paragraph uses the phrase "early days of American animation," which suggests that this was the world before *Snow White*. Let's keep it. Choice B doesn't work because the paragraph states that the short films produced in New York were "low-quality." That doesn't match up with B's statement about high-quality animation. Ditch B. Choice C goes for the same reason—"low-quality" doesn't sound like "inventiveness." Choice D makes a plain statement that we can check. Question 6 helps out here—we decided that the main point of the essay is that *Snow White* was important to animation. That's not what paragraph 3 is about, so D is wrong. The correct answer, then, is A.

In question number 8 you're asked to do a very specific thing: to add a sentence that would "illustrate the emotional connection audiences had with *Snow White*." This sort of question is a lot easier than it first seems because you can use the question itself to eliminate wrong answers. Any answer choice that doesn't deal directly with what the question asks (in this case, emotional audiences) is out immediately. Let's take a look at the answers. Choice F is talking about the money *Snow White* earned, not emotion, so it's gone. Choice G says that people still rent *Snow White*, so it's talking about audiences, but it doesn't get into why people are renting it. The emotional side is missing, so this one is no good. Choice H sounds pretty good. Touching hearts is pretty emotional stuff. We'll keep this one. Choice J is from left field. Who cares what Barrymore went on to do? We want emotional audiences, and this choice doesn't have them. The correct answer is H.

Before we let you off the hook for this chapter, we're going to put you through your paces on one of ACT's favorite topics—brevity. The folks in Iowa City are extraordinarily fond of offering you choices that all say the same thing, but in a variety of forms. Typically, one of the answers will be much shorter and drier than the others. The other choices will be full of colorful language, purple prose, and slang. Guess which one they want you to choose? That's right. The dull one.

As far as the test writers are concerned, good language is clear, concise, focused, and NOT redundant. Keep that in mind as you do the next drill.

But what role do the parents play in the <u>development of the child being raised</u>? There
¹
are many stories of children with indifferent parents, or no parents, doing very well in life. A famous chain of hamburger restaurants was founded by an orphan <u>who did not have parents</u>. There have been
²
presidents whose fathers took <u>no active role in child-rearing</u>. By the same token, there
³
are many parents who tried their best, only to see their children wind up in trouble in life.

The case of two of the sons of John Adams, second president of the United States, is an interesting one to consider in this context. Although known mainly for his political successes, Adams had both success and failure in raising his children <u>from wee babes to strapping young men</u>.
⁴

1. **A.** NO CHANGE
   B. raising up of a child being developed
   C. development of the child
   D. childs rearing

2. **F.** NO CHANGE
   G. whose parents were not around
   H. without parents
   J. OMIT the underlined selection

3. **A.** NO CHANGE
   B. no activity in the rearing of their child's role
   C. no role
   D. OMIT the underlined selection

4. **F.** NO CHANGE
   G. from when they were born until they moved out on their own
   H. through thick and thin, better or worse
   J. OMIT the underlined selection

In question number 1 you have to choose from a number of variations on a theme. That's a sign that ACT is testing whether you can spot redundancies and the most concise way of saying something. In this question "development" and "raised" are pretty close in meaning, so look for a clearer answer than A. Choice B is passive, which is generally wrong, and continues the redundancy. Both C and D drop the redundancy, but D should have an apostrophe to be possessive, so C is correct.

When OMIT is an option, you want to look long and hard at it, because the odds are good that it's the correct answer. This is true in question number 2. Being an orphan means not having parents, so F, G, and H are all redundant. The correct answer is J.

Although you should check OMIT carefully when it is offered, it isn't always right. In question number 3, if you omit the underlined portion, you turn the sentence into a fragment, so cross off D. You can get rid of B, too, because it's "child," not "role" that's supposed to be reared. Choice C is very concise, but doesn't tell us what "role" the father is involved in, so the correct answer is A.

Question number 4 has some very colloquial options as answer choices, and those are nearly always wrong. The question is, can you omit what is underlined and still have a good sentence? Yes, you can, and yes, you should. The correct answer is J.

Step 3:
Ballparking

What Is on the Math Test?

The Math test of the ACT has exactly the same types of problems every time the test is given. You can count on seeing the following assortment of questions:

Pre-Algebra	14
Elementary Algebra	10
Intermediate Algebra	9
Coordinate Geometry	9
Plane Geometry	14
Trigonometry	4

Whenever you choose to take the ACT, this is the breakdown you'll have on your test. What you *don't* know is which questions will be the hard ones and which will be the easy ones. What this breakdown does is tell you what you need to be studying. Because there's no calculus, don't bother with studying calc. Because there are only four trig questions, you probably don't want to spend too much time on trig either.

The bulk of the questions are in geometry and algebra—stuff you probably finished studying in tenth grade. The fact of the matter is, there is a lot of math on the ACT that you last studied before high school. You're going to need to review those topics in order to do well on the test.

Remember Your Calculator

You are allowed to use a calculator on the ACT's math questions. Sometimes it will be useful, and sometimes it won't. They say that every question on the test can be done without a calculator, and they're right. However, doing the test this way is no fun at all, so remember to bring your calculator.

If you don't have your calculator handy right now, you should. You'll need it to do the math questions in this book. Remember: Always have your calculator when doing ACT math problems.

Keep in mind that not all calculators are permitted for use on the ACT. You can check their website (www.act.org) for the specifics. Basically, if your calculator has a Computer Algebra System (such as the TI-89, HP-40G, and Casio CFX-9970G do), you can't use it on the ACT. Don't think that you'll be able to sneak a banned calculator by the proctors, either. ACT has been pushing its proctors to crack down, and they are checking more carefully than they used to.

Don't Get Stuck

The math on the ACT is not in a set order of difficulty. That means there are some easy problems toward the beginning of the test and there are some hard problems toward the end of the test. This is not the way things are arranged on the SAT, which always has the easiest questions first and the hardest questions last.

Although the first 20 math questions on the ACT are generally easier than those that come later, you can count on seeing some easy questions among the final 10 questions as well. There are also usually a few pretty tough questions early on in the test. When you take the Math test, don't let yourself get stuck. The worst thing you can do is spend a long time on a hard question when there are still easy questions left to be done. The way to avoid this is to use a two-pass system.

The Two-Pass System

Do the Math test in two passes. On your first pass through, deal with two types of questions: those you are sure you can do, and those you know are impossible for you. Also, circle and skip problems you think you can do but that will take some work. Once you've worked your way through the entire test in this way (finishing your first pass), you're going to come back and work on the problems you circled and skipped.

You want to take the test this way so that you don't miss any of the easy points. All questions have the same value, and you don't get bonus points for struggling successfully to answer a really tough question, so you want to make sure you get to every question that you know how to do. Because they don't put all the questions that you know how to do in one place, the only way to find them is to use this two-pass system.

On the first pass you do the easy questions because they're easy. Get all the easy points right away! You also "do" the impossible ones because they're impossible. Let's say you can't do trig graphing, and on your first pass you come to a trig graphing question. Spending any time on this question would be a waste, so you don't want to circle it for later. You also don't want to leave it blank on your answer sheet, because you might get lucky and guess correctly (remember that there's no penalty for wrong answers). So, randomly put an answer down for it and move on, looking for more questions you know how to do.

On the second pass go back and work on the questions you circled in the first pass. Spending time on questions you think you may be able to figure out is much wiser than taking a ten-minute nap at the end of the section. When you have five minutes left, stop and put an answer down for every question you're not going to get to.

Two-Pass Technique

Do the questions you are sure of; guess on the ones that stump you. Circle everything else.

Go back and work on the circled questions.

Don't Live in the Past

The ACT is constantly changing. The test writers look at the curricula of American high schools and adjust their test to reflect what's being taught. They also try to keep the math questions a step ahead of the calculators. One way to do that is to ban certain calculators that can tear algebra questions to pieces (see "Remember Your Calculator" in this chapter). Another way is to write theoretical abstract questions you simply cannot put into a calculator.

We take the ACT every time it's given to see how the test is shifting. ACT has pretty much eliminated simple plug-n-chug questions from the Math test. We're seeing three major changes taking place. First, there are more long word questions with elaborate setups. Second, ACT is starting to put more useless information into the questions. Finally, ACT is asking more theoretical questions (like what it takes to define a plane) on recent exams.

All of these changes force you to do more thinking about the mathematical concepts behind the problems and prevent you from just tossing numbers into your calculator on every question. Keep this in mind during your two-pass attack.

The Big Technique: Ballparking

As you already know, every math question on the ACT has one right answer and four wrong answers. Your job is to eliminate those wrong answers and pick the right one. When the people who write the ACT are constructing a math question, the first answer they come up with is the right answer. Then, they build the wrong answers by working the problem and making the sorts of mistakes that a careless (or rushing) student might make. The wrong answers they get are what they use as the wrong answers on the test. That's why when you screw up on a question, you frequently find your wrong answer listed. Sneaky, eh?

In order to reduce the chance of this happening, and in order to help you get rid of some wrong answers on questions you're not exactly sure how to do (which will help you guess better), you're going to use a technique we call Ballparking.

Ballparking is the name for the process of reading a question, figuring out roughly what the right answer will be (without actually working the problem), and then crossing out any answers that are too big or too small.

For example, if a question says that the price of something increases 20 percent from $300, you can immediately cross out anything less than $300, because the price is going up, not down. You could also get rid of anything bigger than $600, because it goes up only 20 percent, which is much less than doubling.

Ballparking will rarely eliminate all four wrong answers, but it will frequently eliminate two or more wrong answers, and that's a real help. Keep in mind that you can't use Ballparking on any questions that have variables in the answer choices, only on questions that have numbers in the answers. Try it out on these problems. (Don't work them out—just practice eliminating answers that are too large or too small for right now.)

23. A pair of running shoes, regularly priced at $75.00, is marked down 20% for summer clearance. If sales tax of 8% is tacked on to the purchase price, how much will Mike pay for these shoes during the sale?

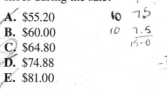

   A. $55.20
   B. $60.00
   C. $64.80
   D. $74.88
   E. $81.00

3. A rectangle has a length of 7 inches and an area of 56 inches. What is its width?

   A.   392
   B.   49
   C.   21
   D.   8
   E.   7

In question number 23 you know that the shoes will cost less than $75, and because they're being marked down by 20%, they'll be at least $10 cheaper. So, you should eliminate D and E right away. Twenty percent of 75 has to be less than 20 (because 20% of 100 is 20), so A, $55.20, is too low. That leaves you with B and C, and if you don't know how to do percentages, you now have a fifty-fifty chance of getting this right anyway.

In question number 3 you can quickly eliminate A and B because they are too large. Area is found by multiplying length and width, and 7 times either of those answers will be way bigger than 56.

Although you don't need to worry about doing these right now (we'll cover both of these topics later on), we'll tell you the answers: Question number 23 is C and question number 3 is D.

Percentages

You can count on seeing plenty of percent questions on the ACT. Fortunately for you, ACT very rarely tests percent change, so you don't have to worry about that. All you have to be able to do is solve basic percent questions. There are two things we're going to teach you for percent questions: the 10 Percent Rule and Translation.

The 10 Percent Rule

The 10 Percent Rule is a quick and dirty way to estimate percentages. We could have used it on question 23 in the Ballparking section. To get 10 percent of any number, take the decimal point and move it one place to the left. So, if you want 10 percent of 225, move the decimal point over (it's after the 5, even though it's not written) and you get 22.5. This method lets you get 1 percent of something quickly, too. Just move the decimal point twice. So, 1 percent of 225 would be 2.25. This is a great way to figure out the right tip in restaurants, by the way. If you wanted to leave a 15 percent tip on a bill of $36, you would first find 10 percent using this method, then divide that by 2 to get 5 percent. Add them together and there's the tip:

10 percent is $3.60, and 5 percent is $1.80, so 15 percent is $5.40.

Translation

The biggest problem most people have with percent questions is setting them up properly. The way to deal with this is to use the following table to *translate* English into math, which will allow you to calculate whatever percent it is you're looking for.

%	divide by 100 (/100)
is, are, will be	=
of	times (multiply)
what, some amount	x, y, z, or any other variable
what percent	$\dfrac{x}{100}$

Here's an example: What is 20 percent of 150? Translate this to $x = \dfrac{20}{100} \times 150$. Solve it, and you'll find that $x = 30$. Remember to use your calculator once you have set up the problems!

Use the 10 Percent Rule and Translation on the following questions.

17. Brockton High School is having a speech contest for the 11th and 12th grades. If 15% of the 360 juniors and 12% of the 300 seniors have decided to enter the contest, how many of Brockton's students will take part in the contest?

    A. 37
    B. 36
    C. 54
    D. 90
    E. 99

25. Kohn's Music Center is selling guitars for $220, which is 80% of the original price. How much did these guitars originally sell for?

    A. $300
    B. $275
    C. $240
    D. $200
    E. $176

18. A team played 45 games and won 18 of them. If there were no ties, what percentage of the games did the team win, to the nearest hundredth?

F. 0.40
G. 2.50
H. 18.00
J. 27.00
K. 40.00

In question number 17 you're trying to find out how many students are entering the contest. To do that, you need to figure out how many juniors are entering and how many seniors are entering. Then add the results together. Let's do some Ballparking first to eliminate partial answers. Because of the 10 Percent Rule, you can figure that there will be more than 30 juniors and more than 30 seniors participating, because 10 percent of 360 is 36 and 10 percent of 300 is 30. That means we'll have at least 60 students total. Eliminate A, B, and C, because they're too small.

Now, figure out the exact numbers. First, juniors. We want to know what is 15 percent of 360. Translate that into math and you get $x = \frac{15}{100} \times 360$. That works out to $x = 54$. Now the seniors. What is 12 percent of 300? Translate that into $y = \frac{12}{100} \times 300$. You can solve this to find $y = 36$. Add the juniors to the seniors and you get a total of 90 students, choice D.

In question number 25 you have to find out what the original price is from the discounted price. This will be tough to ballpark, but we can be sure that the right answer will be more than the discounted price, so let's see if there are any choices that we can cross out. Yes—both D and E are too small, so get rid of them. Even if we go no further, we now have a one-in-three chance of getting this one right.

The thing to do on this type of problem is set up the question in English and then translate it into math. If you can do that, the rest is very simple. The question for Translation is 220 is 80 percent of how much? Using the Translation chart, that works out to be $220 = \frac{80}{100} \times g$. Now you've got an equation with one variable, which you can solve. You should get $g = 275$ as your answer, or B.

In question 18, you can do some great Ballparking. The 10 Percent Rule tells you that 10 percent of 45 is 4.5. Because the team won 18 games—way more than 4.5—you can immediately eliminate F and G as too small. Now get set to translate and calculate.

Translate the following into math: 18 is what percent of 45? That translates into $18 = \frac{q}{100} \times 45$. Work this out and you'll find $q = 40$, which is choice K.

Do You Speak Math?

Although almost everyone believes that the ACT Math test is all about numbers and calculations, the truth of the matter is that it's also a huge vocabulary test. Think about it: If you don't know what certain mathematical terms mean, like *reciprocal* or *bisect*, you'll never be able to do the questions on the test. On every ACT there are a number of questions that test your knowledge of terms like these—not your calculator prowess.

We're going to review several of the key ACT terms by working through the next three problems.

33. What is the smallest possible product for two positive even integers whose sum is 24?

    A.   0
    B.   23
    C.   24
    D.   44
    E.   144

In order to do this question, you need to know a number of things. First, what's an integer? An *integer* is a number that has no decimal part, like –3 or 0 or 5. Second, what do *even* and *positive* mean? *Even* means divisible by 2, and *positive* means greater than 0 (0 is neither positive nor negative, although it is even). Then there's the issue of product and sum. A *product* is what you get when you multiply two numbers together, and a *sum* is what you get when you add them. See—we told you it was a vocabulary test!

There are a couple of ways to do this question. You could try all pairs of even integers that add up to 24, or you could think about what they are looking for—the smallest product—and let that guide you in your quest. If we want the product to be small, we want the numbers to be small. Well, the smallest even number is 2, and to get 24, you'd have to add 22 to it. The product of 2 and 22 is 44, so D is a possibility. The next smallest even integer is 4, which goes with 20 to make 24. The product of those two is 80, however, which means we're moving in the wrong direction. We'll probably stick with 44, but let's check one other thing out first. Let's try using 12 and 12. The question doesn't say the two even integers have to be different, only that they add up to 24. If we multiply 12 and 12, we get 144. That's also bigger than 44, so we're done. Choice D is the correct answer.

28. Which of the following is equal to the product of x and the square of its reciprocal for all $x < 0$?

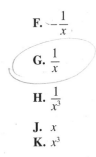

F. $-\dfrac{1}{x}$

G. $\dfrac{1}{x}$

H. $\dfrac{1}{x^3}$

J. x

K. x^3

Once again, vocabulary is the key to getting a question right. We've gone over *product* already, but what about *square* and *reciprocal*? *Square* means to multiply something by itself, so the square of x is $(x)(x)$, or x^2. The reciprocal of something is 1 divided by that something. For example, the reciprocal of x is $\frac{1}{x}$. The reciprocal of $\frac{1}{y^2}$ is $\frac{1}{\frac{1}{y^2}}$, which is the same as y^2.

Now, back to the question. We want the product of x and the square of its reciprocal, so that would be $x\left(\frac{1}{x}\right)^2$. That's the same as $x\left(\frac{1}{x^2}\right)$, which works out to $\frac{x}{x^2}$. Then you can cancel an x and get $\frac{1}{x}$, G. Wait a minute—the question said that x is negative, so shouldn't it be F? No, it shouldn't. The fact that x is negative will automatically make the whole thing negative—there's no need to add an extra negative sign. The correct answer is G.

41. What is the greatest common factor of $18x^2$ and $24x^5$?

$6x^2$

  A. x^2
  B. $2x^2$
  C. $6x^2$
  D. $18x^2$
  E. $24x^5$

Here we have a term from grade school! The greatest common factor of two (or more) things is the largest number that goes into all of them evenly. For example, the greatest common factor of 4, 12, and 24, is 4, because that's the biggest number that goes into all three numbers evenly. Sure, 6 goes into 12 and 24, but it doesn't go into 4, so it's not a factor of 4. Common factors have to go into every element smoothly.

This question is a bit more complicated than that, however, because it involves variables. No problem. The thing to do is deal with the coefficients (the numbers) separately from the variables. It will probably be easier to deal with the variables first.

What's the biggest thing that could go into both x^2 and x^5? If you said x^2, you're right. Eliminate E, but don't pick A yet, because we haven't dealt with the coefficients. Let's do that now. What's the biggest number that goes into both 18 and 24? The only way to figure it out is to try out some numbers. Try numbers from the answers themselves (more on this in the next chapter) because one of them must be right. The number 2 works, so eliminate A, because we're looking for the *greatest* common factor, not just any common factor. The number 6 works, too, so B is out. But 18 doesn't go into 24, so D doesn't work. All we have left is C, which is the correct answer.

Absolute Value

Absolute value is another way of talking about how far something is from zero on a number line. One way of thinking about the absolute value operator, which is the pair of vertical lines in this correctly worked equation $|-2| = 2$, is that it makes everything inside of itself positive. So, while $|-2| = 2$, it's also true that $|2| = 2$. In other words, for every positive answer coming out of an absolute value, there are two possible ways to get there—the negative value being made positive, as we did with -2, or the positive value remaining positive, as happened with 2 when it was inside the absolute value signs. ACT likes to base questions on this aspect of the absolute value operator.

27. What is the sum of the solutions to $|3 - x| + 2 = 6$?

    A. -8
    B. -1
    C. 6
    D. 7
    E. 8

handwritten work in margins

Because there is a variable inside the absolute value bars, there are going to be two solutions to this equation. What you need to do is solve it like a regular equation until you have only the absolute value on one side. Then, set up two equations—one with a positive answer and one with a negative answer—and solve them both. (If this were an inequality, you'd need to flip the inequality sign on the negative answer.)

$|3 - x| + 2 = 6$ First, move the 2 over.

$|3 - x| = 4$ Now, set up your two equations and solve them.

Positive		Negative
$3 - x = 4$	and	$3 - x = -4$
$-x = 1$	and	$-x = -7$
$x = -1$	and	$x = 7$

Now you have the two solutions for the equation. You can check both of them by putting them back into the original equation. Because the question was asking for the sum, add them to get the answer: 6. The correct answer is C. Try the next two on your own.

37. Which of the following represents the range of values which satisfies the inequality $|x - 5| < 3$?

A. $x < -2$ and $x > -8$
B. $x > -2$ and $x < -8$
C. $x > 2$ and $x < 8$
D. $x < 2$ and $x > 8$
E. $x < 3$ and $x > 5$

$x - 5 < 3 \qquad x - 5 > -3$
$+5 \quad +5 \qquad +5 \quad +5$
$x < 8 \qquad x > 2$

43. For what values of x is the equation $|3x| + 5 = 1$ true?

A. -4
B. -2
C. $-\dfrac{4}{3}$
D. 2
E. No values of x satisfy this equation.

$+5 \quad -5$
$\dfrac{3x}{3} = \dfrac{-4}{3}$
$x = \dfrac{4}{3}$

$\dfrac{3x}{3} = \dfrac{-5}{3}$
$x = \dfrac{-5}{3}$

In question number 37 you need to split the job up into the positive and negative solutions. When dealing with an inequality and an absolute value, you must flip the inequality around when doing the negative solution. So, your two equations should look like this:

$$x - 5 < 3 \quad \text{and} \quad x - 5 > -3$$
$$x < 8 \quad \text{and} \quad x > 2$$

Choice C is correct.

In question 43, you need to solve it as usual.

$$|3x| + 5 = 1$$
$$|3x| = -4$$

At this point, you should realize that this is impossible (ACT does ask questions just like this on the exam). What comes out of an absolute value operation can never be negative, so this problem cannot be solved. The correct answer is E.

Recently the writers of the ACT have been asking more and more questions that involve conceptualization instead of calculation. Because ACT allows calculators now, the test writers tend to minimize the calculator-friendly questions.

When you do questions of this sort, it sometimes helps to sketch little diagrams, or visualize the shapes in your head. Most people fall into one of two camps on these questions—they either really like them, or really hate them. The people who like them generally are great at visualizing already. Those who aren't great visualizers can have trouble with this. The way to get better is to practice.

If you aren't good at seeing images in your head, draw as much as you can. Read the problem carefully, and draw what you can from the information they give you. Does the problem describe a triangle or a set of points? Draw that. Does it describe some dimensions or a relationship? Jot that down. Then go to the answers to see if they conform to what the problem tells you. Using POE to get rid of bad answer choices is critical to success on these if you have trouble with them. Ultimately, the more of these you work through, the better you'll be.

So, if you like these kinds of questions, great! And if you don't, keep plugging away at them and you'll get better slowly. Fortunately, the ACT doesn't ask too many questions of this type on each test, so if you have too much difficulty with them, you can skip them and it won't harm your score too much (there are plenty of other questions to work on).

1. If a triangle has one side of length 8, which of the following could be the lengths of the other two sides?

    A. 2 and 10
    B. 3 and 4
    C. 4 and 4
    D. 5 and 8
    E. 6 and 1

2. What is described by the set of all points exactly 2 cm from a given point in space?

    F. A line 2 cm long
    G. An infinitely long cylinder with a radius of 2 cm
    H. A circle with a radius of 2 cm
    J. A sphere with a radius of 2 cm
    K. A double helix of length 2 cm

3. If a sphere is cut by two different planes, dividing it into sections, how many sections is it possible to end up with?

    A. 2 only
    B. 2 or 4 only
    C. 3 only
    D. 3 or 4 only
    E. 2, 3, or 4 only

In question number 1 you can't really use your calculator because there are no equations to use. The question is asking if you understand the rules governing triangles. In this case, what you need to know is that the legs have to be long enough to reach one another. Any leg has to be between the sum and the difference of the other two sides.

For example, in A, the difference in the sides is 8, and the side given in the question is 8, so this won't work. If you draw it, you'll see that you can't make a triangle, only a flat thing with the 10 on the bottom and the 2 and 8 going straight across above it. For B, the sum of 3 and 4 is 7, so the longest third side has to be less than 7 (again, try to draw it), so B is out. Choices C and E are wrong for similar reasons, leaving D. The difference of 5 and 8 is 3, and the sum is 13, so this works.

Question number 2 is purely theoretical. You need to be able to visualize what happens if you have a point and then go 2 cm away from it in every direction. What happens is you make a ball, so the answer is J.

Question number 3 is another visualization problem. If you're a good artist, you might be able to sketch something that helps you. Otherwise, try to think it through slowly, and eliminate choices as you go. You're cutting a sphere with planes, so imagine ways of slicing an orange with a knife. One slice results in two pieces. Then you have to cut what's left, so you know you'll have more than two pieces. Cross off A, B, and E. If you go next to your first cut, you can make three pieces (the orange looks sort of like a weird sandwich). So, C and D are both possibilities. Can you make four pieces? Sure. Have the second cut make an "X" with the first. The answer is D.

Step 4:
Plugging In

Numbers Are Nicer Than Variables

Here's a question for you to read to start off this chapter.

17. Which of the following correctly gives the average of x, $x + 3$, $2x - 5$, and $6x - 1$?

 A. $2x - 5$

 B. $x - \dfrac{3}{4}$

 C. $\dfrac{5}{2}x + \dfrac{9}{4}$

 D. $10x - 3$

 E. $\dfrac{5}{2}x - \dfrac{3}{4}$

If you came across this question while taking the ACT, you might think to yourself, "Gaah! I don't want to do this—there are way too many variables here." Well, we agree with you, so we're going to teach you a way to eliminate all of the variables from this problem and turn it into a simple arithmetic problem. We'll do it by using one of our most powerful techniques—Plugging In.

The Big Technique: Plugging In

What is it about question number 17 that makes it troublesome? It's all those variables, right? If the question were asking you to find the average of four integers, it would be a snap, wouldn't it? So, what you're going to do is make up a value for x and change all the variables into real numbers. Let's use 5 for x and work the problem out.

If $x = 5$, then the question is asking us to find the average of 5, 8, 5, and 29. That's easy enough.

$$\frac{5 + 8 + 5 + 29}{4} = \frac{47}{4} = 11.75$$

The answer is 11.75. Now that you've found the answer, go to the answer choices, plug in 5 for every x (because we picked 5 for x at the beginning, we have to use it all the way through—don't change your value for x in the middle of a problem), and see which answer choice works out to 11.75.

Choice A is $2(5) - 5 = 5$. That's not 11.75, so cross it out. Choice B works out to 5.25—too small; eliminate it. Choice C is $\frac{5}{2}(5) + \frac{9}{4} = 12.5 + 2.25 = 14.75$. That's too big, so cross C out, too. Choice D is 47—way too big. That leaves only E, which works out like this: $\frac{5}{2}(5) + \frac{3}{4} = 12.5 - .75 = 11.75$—exactly what we are looking for! Choice E is the correct answer.

So maybe you're thinking that we got lucky here. Nope, not at all. Plugging In will work on any question with variables in the answer choices. As long as you follow the simple rules, you'll get the right answer on every Plugging In question on the test. Here's how to do it:

Step 1
Pick numbers for all the variables. Write them down above the variables in the question so you keep track of what's what.

Step 2
Solve the question using your numbers. Circle whatever you get. That's the answer, and you're going to match it up with one of the answer choices.

Step 3
Put your numbers into the answer choices and solve them. Find the one that matches your answer from step 2. Always check every answer choice. If you get more than one that works, just use a different set of numbers and try again (this doesn't happen very often, but we'll demonstrate how to handle it later in this chapter anyway).

That's all there is to it.

Pick Easy Numbers

Remember that you still have to do some math when you're plugging in, so pick numbers that are going to make your life easier. We picked 5 in that average question, not 137.92. Yes, it would have worked if we had picked 137.92 (go ahead and try it out if you don't believe us), but why make life so hard? By picking 5, we kept the math simple and barely worked up a sweat finding the right answer.

Keeping that in mind, then, take a look at this:

23. If $q = \dfrac{3(s-5)}{t}$, then what is s in terms of q and t?

A. $qt + 8$

B. $\dfrac{8q}{t}$

C. $\dfrac{qt+5}{3}$

D. $\dfrac{qt}{3} + 5$

E. $\dfrac{3qt}{5}$

(handwritten:)
$q \dfrac{3s-15}{t}$

$\dfrac{3s-15}{t} = \dfrac{qt+15}{3}$

$s = \dfrac{qt+5}{3}$

Here we've got three different variables. No problem—plugging in will handle this easily. Whenever you have multiple variables, you want to plug in for the variable that's buried in the middle of stuff first and work your way out to the other ones. That means starting with s here. If we make $s = 10$, the top of that fraction will be 15. Make $t = 5$, and that will make $q = 3$.

The question is asking what s is, so circle 10, because that is what we plugged in for s. Now it's on to the answer choices.

A. $(3)(5) + 8 = 23$ Nope.

B. $\dfrac{(8)(3)}{5} = \dfrac{24}{5}$ Nope.

C. $\dfrac{(5)(3) + 5}{3} = \dfrac{20}{5}$ Nope.

D. $\dfrac{(5)(3)}{3} + 5 = 10$ Yes. But always check all five answers.

E. $\dfrac{(3)(5)(3)}{5} = 9$ Nope.

Choice D is our answer. So when do you want to plug in? Every single time you can. It's a foolproof way of getting the questions right, and that's what it's all about on the ACT, right? Right.

Try to plug in on this question before reading the explanation that follows:

31. Which of the following is equal to $\dfrac{2}{x} - \dfrac{2}{1-x}$ for all $x \neq 0$ and $x \neq 1$?

A. 0
B. 2
C. $\dfrac{4}{x}$
D. $\dfrac{2}{x(x-1)}$
E. $\dfrac{2(1-2x)}{x(1-x)}$

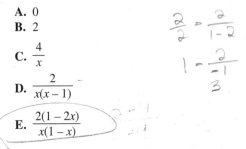

Did you do the question? Don't start reading this explanation unless you actually picked a number for x and plugged in until you got the answer. Plugging In, like all of our techniques, will work only if you practice it.

Okay, let's plug in 4 for x. The equation then works out like this:

$$\frac{2}{4} - \frac{2}{1-4} = \frac{1}{2} - \left(-\frac{2}{3}\right) = \frac{1}{2} + \frac{2}{3} = \frac{7}{6}$$

So, now it's on to the answer choices. Right away, A and B are out. If you look more closely, you'll notice that you need a 7 in your numerator. Choices C and D can also be eliminated. Let's plug in for E to make sure our target matches.

E. $\quad\dfrac{2(1-2(4))}{4(1-4)} = \dfrac{-14}{-12} = \dfrac{7}{6}$ YES!!!

If you didn't get E when you plugged in, go back and check your math. You made a miscalculation at some point. It's important to find out where so that you see what type of mistake you tend to make. That way, you'll be more sensitive to avoiding similar missteps in the future.

0 and 1 Are Okay

Although you need to be careful about plugging in 0 and 1 (this is why you always check all five answer choices), there are certain types of Plugging In questions for which 0 and 1 are great to use. Any question that has variables being raised to powers is going to be a great candidate for plugging in 0 or 1. Here's an example:

19. For all $x > 0$, which of the following is equivalent to $\dfrac{5x^3 + 22x^2 - 19}{x+4}$?

A. $5x^2 + 2x - 8$

B. $5x^2 + 2x - 13$

C. $5x^2 + 2x - 8 + \dfrac{13}{x+4}$

D. $5x^2 + 2x + 8 + \dfrac{13}{x+4}$

E. $5x^2 - 2x + \dfrac{13}{x+4}$

Sure, you might be able to do this with synthetic division, but plugging in is going to be much, much faster and less painful. Let's use $x = 0$. The equation in the question immediately becomes $\frac{-19}{4}$, or -4.75. Now let's check the answer choices.

A. -8 Nope.

B. -13 Nope.

C. $-8 + \dfrac{13}{4} = -4.75$ That's what we want.

D. $-8 + \dfrac{13}{4}$ This will be positive. We want negative.
Don't bother working it out any further.

E. $\dfrac{13}{4}$ Also positive. Also wrong.

Plugging in 0 or 1 on this type of question is lightning-fast and just about foolproof. Try it yourself on the next question:

42. What is the simplified form of $\dfrac{2x-5}{x} + \dfrac{4}{x^2}$ for all $x \neq 0$?

F. $\dfrac{1}{x^2}$

G. $\dfrac{2x-1}{x^2}$

H. $\dfrac{2x-1}{x(x-1)}$

J. $\dfrac{2x^2-5x+4}{x^2}$

K. $\dfrac{2x^2+5x+4}{x^2}$

We can't use 0 here, because the question rules it out, so you should have plugged in 1 for x. If you do that, here's how the equation in the question works out:

$$\frac{2x-5}{x}+\frac{4}{x^2}=\frac{2-5}{1}+\frac{4}{1}=-3+4=1$$

So, 1 is the answer we're looking for. Circle it, and head to the answer choices.

F. $\frac{1}{x^2}=1$ Yep. But always check all five answers.

G. $\frac{2x-1}{x^2}=\frac{1}{1}=1$ Hmm. This works, too.

H. $\frac{2x-1}{x(x-1)}=\frac{1}{1(0)}$ This won't equal 1, so cross it out.

J. $\frac{2x^2-5x+4}{x^2}=\frac{2-5+4}{1}=\frac{1}{1}$ This works, too.

K. $\frac{2x^2+5x+4}{x^2}=\frac{2+5+4}{1}=\frac{11}{1}$ Nope. Cross it out.

When more than one answer choice works, as has happened here, simply plug in another number for x. Let's use 2. When we do that, this is how the equation in the question works out.

$$\frac{2x-5}{x}+\frac{4}{x^2}=\frac{4-5}{2}+\frac{4}{4}=-\frac{1}{2}+1=0.5$$

So, it's back to the answer choices, looking for 0.5, but we check only F, G, and J. Choices H and K were eliminated already, so there's no need to try them again.

F. $\frac{1}{x^2}=\frac{1}{4}$ Nope. Cross it out.

G. $\frac{2x-1}{x^2}=\frac{4-1}{4}=\frac{3}{4}=0.75$ Nope. Cross it out.
Looks good for J.

J. $\frac{2x^2-5x+4}{x^2}=\frac{8-10+4}{4}=\frac{2}{4}=0.5$ Yep, that's the
right answer for this one.

Geometry Plugging In

Plugging In is a hugely powerful technique (on one recent ACT we counted more than ten questions that you could do with Plugging In), and you should use it at every available opportunity. This means don't use it just on algebra questions—use it on geometry questions, too. Whenever you have variables in the answers, plug in!

Plugging In works on geometry questions the same way that it works on other questions. You plug in your numbers, solve for the answer, and then check the answer choices. Remember not to violate any of the rules of geometry, though—no triangles with 300 degrees or squares with five sides!

14. A triangle with a base of 4 and a height of 6 has both of these dimensions increased by z. What is the area of the new triangle?

    F. $12 + z$

    G. $12 + \dfrac{z}{2}$

    H. $\dfrac{z^2}{2}$

    J. $\dfrac{z^2}{2} + 5$

    K. $\dfrac{z^2}{2} + 5z + 12$

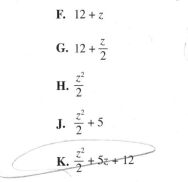

You know how this works by now. Let's use 2 for z. We need to find the new area. The new base is $4 + 2 = 6$ and the new height is $6 + 2 = 8$, so the new area is $\frac{1}{2}(6)(8) = 24$. On to the answers.

F. $12 + z = 12 + 2 = 14$ Nope.

G. $12 + \frac{z}{2} = 12 + 1 = 13$ Nope.

H. $\frac{z^2}{2} = \frac{4}{2} = 2$ Nope.

J. $\frac{z^2}{2} + 5 = \frac{4}{2} + 5 = 7$ Nope.

K. $\frac{z^2}{2} + 5z + 12 = \frac{4}{2} + 10 + 12 = 24$ That's what we're looking for.

PITA!

No, it's not snack time. PITA stands for Plugging In The Answers, another type of Plugging In problem that you'll find on the ACT.

PITA is a technique you can use when the ACT tells you a little story and then asks you how many or how much. All the answers are real numbers, and only one of them works in the story ACT told (of course—otherwise there'd be more than one right answer). So, what you're going to do on this type of question is try the answers out in the little story. Plug the Answers Into The story. (Okay, so that way it spells PAIT, but you get the idea.)

Here's how it works on a real problem:

40. David, Heidi, and Shawn are shopping for a gift for Cindy. If David pays $\frac{1}{3}$ as much as Heidi does, Shawn and Heidi pay the same amount, and the gift costs $210, how much did David pay? (Disregard taxes when figuring your answer.)

    F. $30
    G. $70
    H. $90
    J. $140
    K. $180

When using PITA, you want to start with the middle answer choice. Because the answer choices are always listed in ascending order, if the middle choice is too big or too small, you can immediately cross off two more wrong answers above or below it. Always label the answer choices before you start solving the problem, and work horizontally so you can easily see what to do on later answer choices. Let's try it on this one. We know the gift costs $210 total, and we're looking for what David paid, so label the answers "David" and then start working on H. Because we know David paid $\frac{1}{3}$ of what Heidi did, and Heidi and Shawn each paid the same amount, we'll put Heidi and Shawn next. The last thing you'll need is the total. Because David pays $\frac{1}{3}$ of what Heidi does, you should start solving by tripling 90 (David's amount in H) to get 270. Put that under both Heidi and Shawn because the question says they paid the same amount. Add the three together and see if it equals 210 (the amount given in the problem).

You should write it like this:

		David	Heidi	Shawn	Total	210?
	F.	$30				
	G.	$70				
Start:	**H.**	$90	270	270	630	NO WAY!
	J.	$140				
	K.	$180				

Okay. Choice H is way too big, so J and K are out, too. Cross them out. Now we can work on G or F. Let's try G next.

		David	Heidi	Shawn	Total	210?
	F.	$30				
	G.	$70	210	210	490	Nope.
Start:	~~**H.** $90~~		270	270	630	
	~~J. $140~~					
	~~**K.** $180~~					

At this point, you're done. Choice G doesn't work, so F must be right. You can check it if you want to.

	David	Heidi	Shawn	Total	210?
F.	30	90	90	210	Yes!

PITA works very well on questions that ask you to determine what point fits a given equation, too.

35. Which of the following points lies on the perimeter of the circle given by the equation $(x - 2)^2 + (y + 5)^2 = 16$?

   A. (2,–5)
   B. (2,–1)
   C. (–2,5)
   D. (–2,1)
   E. ($\sqrt{2}, \sqrt{5}$)

To use PITA on a question like this, try the points out in the equation given. Unlike when you choose your own number with regular Plugging In, only one of them will work, so stop when you find one that does.

A. (2,–5) $(2 - 2)^2 + (-5 + 5)^2 = 0 + 0 \neq 16$ No good.
B. (2,–1) $(2 - 2)^2 + (-1 + 5)^2 = 0 + (4)^2 = 16$
   This looks good. We're done.
C. (–2,5)
D. (–2,1)
E. $(\sqrt{2}, \sqrt{5})$

Because B worked, there was no point trying the three answer choices remaining. Only one will work, so once you've found it, you're done.

Try PITA on your own on this next question (remember to start with C so you can use POE).

37. A cookie recipe calls for flour and sugar to be combined in a 9:1 ratio. If the recipe yields 3 dozen cookies for each pound of this flour and sugar mix, how many pounds of sugar will be needed to make 27 dozen cookies?

A. $\dfrac{9}{10}$

B. $\dfrac{81}{10}$

C. 9

D. 81

E. 27

Work it out on your own before continuing.

Here's what you should have:

	Sugar	Flour	Total	Cookies	27 Doz?
A.	$\dfrac{9}{10}$	$\dfrac{81}{10}$	$\dfrac{90}{10}$	27 Doz	Yep
B.	$\dfrac{81}{10}$	$\dfrac{90}{10}$	$\dfrac{729}{10}$	243 Doz	No
C.	9	81	90	270 Doz	No
D.	81				
E.	27				

Choice A is the correct answer because it works out to make 27 dozen cookies. Because the flour to sugar ratio is 9:1, you find the amount of flour by multiplying the sugar by 9. Add them to get the total number of pounds. The question says that each pound of mix makes 3 dozen cookies, so multiply pounds by 3 to get the number of dozens that you could make from that much mix.

Step 5:
Staying
Balanced

Solving for x

Much of the math on the ACT is dependent on manipulation of equations, as we've already seen. Manipulating equations, or solving for x, is a skill you can't live without on this test. Fortunately, we're well equipped to take you through everything you need to know about solving for x on the ACT.

There are two basic types of solving for x questions you will find on the ACT. In one, all the values for the variables are given and you have to work out the math. This is by far the easier type. In the other, you are given an equation and have to solve for the variables on your own. We'll start off with the first type.

8. What is the value of $2x^2 - 3x + 2$ when $x = -2$?

   F. −12
   G. 0
   H. 4
   J. 10
   K. 16

In this kind of question, all of the pieces are given to you. All you need to do is the math—carefully. ACT likes to use negatives, so keep your eyes open for those. Remember to set up the problem on paper before you begin stabbing at your calculator. You should recopy the equation with −2 in place of every x, like so:

$$2(-2)^2 - 3(-2) + 2$$

When solving an equation, take care of calculations inside parentheses first; then apply exponents. We don't have any calculations happening inside parentheses here, so we'll do the exponent first and get this:

$$2(4) - 3(-2) + 2$$

(Remember that a negative times a negative gives a positive.)

Next, handle multiplication and division, from left to right.

$$8 - (-6) + 2$$

Now we are subtracting a negative number, which is the same as adding a positive number.

$$8 + 6 + 2$$

Now do the addition, which will give you

$$16$$

This is choice K. The other answer choices all represent miscalculations, mostly dealing with mistakes in handling the negative stuff.

Here's another one, with more variables:

13. What is the value of $3(a)^2 + \dfrac{2b}{c} - \dfrac{a}{c}$ if $a = -2$, $b = 3$, and $c = 4$?

 A. -11
 B. -10
 C. 12
 D. 13
 E. 14

Solve this one in just the same way. Here are the steps:

$$3(-2)^2 + \frac{2(3)}{4} - \frac{(-2)}{4}$$

$$3(4) + \frac{2(3)}{4} - \frac{(-2)}{4}$$

$$12 + \frac{6}{4} - \frac{(-2)}{4}$$

$$12 + \frac{6}{4} + \frac{2}{4}$$

$$14$$

Choice E is the correct answer.

The Big Technique: Don't Tip the Scales

The more difficult kind of solving-for-*x* question asks you to find the value of *x* rather than just giving it to you. The key to success is remembering that everything you do on one side of the equation must be done on the other side of the equation. Pretend that the equation is a perfectly balanced scale that must stay that way. If you take 2 off one side, you must take 2 off the other side. If you add 4 to one side, you must add 4 to the other side. The same thing goes for multiplying and dividing. Whatever you do to one side must be done to the other.

11. If $\dfrac{2x + 5}{3} = 5$, what is the value of *x*?

    A. -5

    B. $\dfrac{3}{2}$

    C. $\dfrac{5}{3}$

    D. 5

    E. 10

Here's how to solve this. The first thing you always want to do is to get rid of any fractions. Fractions are bad because they frequently cause people to get things wrong, so they should be eliminated whenever possible. The way to get rid of fractions is to multiply both sides by whatever's in the bottom of the fractions until all the fractions are gone. Because the bottom of the fraction here is 3, that means we'll start by multiplying everything (on both sides) by 3.

$$3\left(\frac{2x + 5}{3} = 5\right)$$

$$2x + 5 = 15$$

The next step is to get the *x* terms on one side and the numbers on the other side. We already have all the *x* terms together on the left, so all we need to do is move that 5 from the left to the right. To do that, we'll have to subtract 5 from both sides. (Never ever subtract from one side and add to the other—that would unbalance the scale.)

$$(2x + 5) - 5 = (15) - 5$$

$$2x = 10$$

Finally, we have to get rid of the 2 stuck on the x. The $2x$ means 2 times x. The opposite of multiplying is dividing, so to get rid of the 2, we have to divide both sides by 2.

$$\frac{2x}{2} = \frac{10}{2}$$

$$x = 5$$

The answer is D.

12. If $2p + 5 - p = 8$, what is the value of p?

F. −1
G. 1
H. 3
J. $\frac{13}{3}$
K. 13

Because there are no fractions in this one, start by combining the p terms.

$$2p + 5 - p = 8$$

$$p + 5 = 8$$

Then move the 5 over.

$$(p + 5) - 5 = 8 - 5$$

$$p = 3$$

The answer is H.

Inequalities

Inequalities are handled almost exactly the same way as equalities (the equations we've been talking about so far in this chapter), with one difference.

When you multiply or divide by a negative number, you must flip the inequality sign.

In all other respects everything is done in exactly the same way as when solving for x. Get rid of the fractions. Get all the x terms together and all the numbers together on opposite sides of the inequality sign. Divide through to get x by itself. All of that is still the same. So let's try it.

17. Which of the following correctly gives the full range of values for x in the inequality $3(x-2) \geq (2x+5) - 3$?

   A. $x \geq \dfrac{8}{5}$

   B. $x \leq \dfrac{8}{5}$

   C. $x \geq 4$

   D. $x \geq 8$

   E. $x \leq 8$

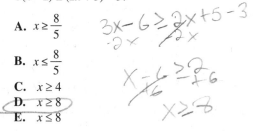

To solve this, approach it just like an equality problem, remembering that if you need to multiply or divide by a negative, you must flip the sign. So, first we'll multiply the 3 on the left through the parentheses.

$$3(x-2) \geq (2x+5) - 3$$

$$3x - 6 \geq (2x+5) - 3$$

Then we'll combine everything on the right side.

$$3x - 6 \geq 2x + 2$$

Now we can bring the x terms together and the numbers together.

$$x \geq 8$$

There's our answer. Choice D is correct.

Number Lines

You may have to deal with questions involving number lines on the ACT, so you need to know how they work. The only tricky thing here is knowing the difference between an open circle and a closed circle.

Open circle means < or >.
Closed circle means ≤ or ≥.

Knowing how this works is a great POE tool, too. You can never change from < to ≥ in a question, so whichever sign is in the question must be in the answer choice. You can eliminate any answers that don't match up immediately.

24. Which of the following correctly represents the solution to $-5 \le x - 2 \le 2$?

$-3 \le x \le 4$

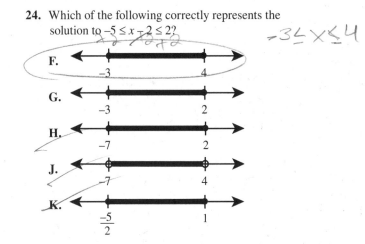

F. [number line with closed circles at -3 and 4]

G. [number line with closed circles at -3 and 2]

H. [number line with closed circles at -7 and 2]

J. [number line with open circles at -7 and 4]

K. [number line with closed circles at $-\frac{5}{2}$ and 1]

We can eliminate J right away, because it has open circles. Solving for x in this one takes no time—just add 2 to everything to get $-3 \le x \le 4$. The right answer, then, is F.

Quadratics and Factoring

Factoring quadratic equations is largely a matter of trial and error combined with some educated guessing. It helps to be able to find the factors of a number pretty quickly. There are three situations you can have when factoring a simple quadratic equation. Knowing what they mean is key to factoring the equation correctly.

If you have an equation like $x^2 + 7x + 12$, in which both operations are addition, you know that it will factor to $(x + something)(x + something)$. If you have an equation in which there is a minus and then a plus, like $x^2 - 5x + 6$, then it will factor to $(x - something)(x - something)$. Finally, if you have an equation in which the last operation is minus, like $x^2 + 7x - 12$, it must factor to $(x + something)(x - something)$.

The whole problem then becomes knowing how to factor. Look at the factors of the last number in the quadratic along with the middle number. The difference or sum of the factors of the last number must equal the middle number, so that's where we'll start. Let's factor $x^2 + 7x + 12$.

$$x^2 + 7x + 12$$

First, set up the final form.

$$(x + \ )(x + \ )$$

Then, think of the factors of 12: 1 and 12, 2 and 6, 3 and 4. Which pair adds up to 7 (the number in the middle)? 3 and 4, right? That's the answer.

$$x^2 + 7x + 12 \text{ factors to}$$
$$(x + 4)(x + 3)$$

How about $x^2 - 5x + 6$? We know it will factor to $(x - \ )(x - \ )$ because of the minus followed by a plus. What factors of 6 add up to 5? 3 and 2. That's the answer.

$$x^2 - 5x + 6$$
$$(x - 2)(x - 3)$$

Finally, let's do $x^2 - 3x - 10$. The minus at the end tells us it will work out to something like $(x + \ )(x - \ )$. The factors of 10 need to have a difference of 3. That would be 5 and 2. Because the middle term is −3, we need 5 to be the factor in the equation with the minus sign.

$$x^2 - 3x - 10$$
$$(x + 2)(x - 5)$$

You can check any of these by using FOIL which is a way of remembering how to multiply the factors. It stands for First, Outer, Inner, Last. (Some graphing calculators will even FOIL for you these days.) *First* means multiply the first terms in each set of parentheses. Here, that's the two x's. *Outer* is the outer two terms, here, the first x and the −5. *Inner* and *Last* work the same way. Then you add everything up. Let's take a look at an example.

39. If $3x^2 - 5x - 2 = 0$, what are the values of x?

  A. $-\dfrac{1}{3}$ and $\dfrac{1}{2}$

  B. $-\dfrac{1}{3}$ and 2

  C. $\dfrac{1}{3}$ and 1

  D. $\dfrac{1}{3}$ and 2

  E. 1 and 2

To answer this question, we're going to have to factor the quadratic and see what we get. Because there is that minus sign at the end, we know it's going to look something like $(x -)(x +)$ when we're done. The 3 on the x^2 term is going to be in the mix as well. It will multiply against one of the factors of 2 to let us get a difference of 5 (the middle term). The factors of 2 are 1 and 2, and to get a difference of 5, the 3 must be multiplied against the 2. Because we have −5 in the middle term, the 2 needs to be in the factor with the minus and the 3 in the one with the plus, like this:

$$(3x + 1)(x - 2)$$

To figure out what values of x solve the equation, then, set each factor equal to zero and solve it.

$$(3x + 1) = 0 \qquad (x - 2) = 0$$
$$3x = -1 \qquad\quad x = 2$$

$$x = -\frac{1}{3}$$

The answer is B. If you got stuck, you could also have used PITA here. Let's try one more:

7. For all x, $(2x - 5)(5x + 1)$ is equivalent to:

    A. $7x - 4$
    B. $7x^2 + 3x - 5$
    C. $10x^2 - 5$
    D. $10x^2 - 23x - 5$
    E. $10x^2 + 27x - 5$

$$10x^2 + 2x - 25x - 5$$
$$10x^2 - 23x - 5$$

Here you have to use FOIL:

First:	$2x \times 5x = 10x^2$
Outer:	$2x \times 1 = 2x$
Inner:	$-5 \times 5x = -25x$
Last:	$-5 \times 1 = -5$

Add them up. You should get $10x^2 - 23x - 5$, which is choice D.

Proportions

Proportions allow you to project a relationship between two things onto a different scale. For example, if it takes 20 minutes to walk 1.5 miles, you can use proportions to figure out how long it would take to walk 17 miles, or how far you would walk in 45 minutes.

The way to do this is to set up two fractions and set them equal to each other. On one side you have the relationship that is given (20 minutes for 1.5 miles, in our example), and on the other you have the relationship you're trying to figure out. Always keep the same units on the top of each fraction. Don't put minutes over miles on the left side and miles over minutes on the right, in other words. It's a good idea to note on the side which unit you want to have on the top and which you want on the bottom. Here's how to do it for this example:

$$\frac{\text{minutes}}{\text{miles}} \qquad \frac{20}{1.5} = \frac{x}{17}$$

Cross multiply to get $1.5x = 340$. So, $x = 226.66$. It would take 226.66 minutes to walk 17 miles at this rate. You could figure out the distance covered in 45 minutes in the same manner.

$$\frac{\text{minutes}}{\text{miles}} \qquad \frac{20}{1.5} = \frac{45}{x}$$

This becomes $20x = 67.5$, so $x = 3.375$. You would walk 3.375 miles in 45 minutes.

Proportions don't come up with only time and distance. You can use them for comparing any two measurements. Take a look at the following problem:

18. If it takes Antonia 45 minutes to make 18 cherry tarts, how many hours will it take her to make 60 cherry tarts if she maintains the same pace?

  F. 1
  G. 1.5
  H. 2.5
  J. 4.5
  K. 150

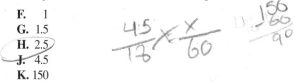

The nasty twist in this problem is that the time is given in minutes, but the answer ACT wants is in hours. You can convert minutes to hours at the beginning or the end—it doesn't matter—but you can't forget to convert. The nonconverted answer is definitely going to be one of the wrong answer choices.

Let's convert at the end. We'll put minutes on top in our calculations.

$$\frac{\text{minutes}}{\text{tarts}} \qquad \frac{45}{18} = \frac{x}{60}$$

This becomes $18x = 2,700$. So, $x = 150$. But that's the answer in minutes. To convert to hours, divide by 60 and you'll get 2.5, or H. Take a look at K—there's the unconverted amount.

Step 6:
Use the Figures

Geometry

Twenty-three of the questions on the ACT Math test are geometry questions of some type. That's more than one-third of the questions on the test. Your ability to handle the geometry on the ACT can make or break you. Fortunately, the writers of the ACT restrict themselves to fairly basic geometry concepts that fall into four major groups. You're not going to see any proofs on the test, and you'll rarely have to deal with anything in three dimensions.

The vast majority of the geometry questions fall into these four categories: angles, perimeters, areas, and coordinate geometry. ACT doesn't give you any of the formulas, so you need to have them memorized. We'll review all of the important ones in this chapter.

The figures on the test are almost always drawn to scale, so you want to be sure to ballpark whenever you can. This will eliminate lots of answers that don't make any sense.

Angles

To do angle questions, you need to know how many degrees there are in basic figures such as the triangle, quadrilateral, and circle, and how parallel lines work. We'll start off with the parallel lines and quadrilaterals and leave the triangles and circles for last.

Any straight line has 180 degrees on each side of it. When you have parallel lines cut by a third line (known as a *transversal*), those lines will make eight angles. The neat thing about these eight angles is that there are really only two different types of angles created—Big and Little.

All of the Big angles are the same size, and all of the Little angles are the same size. In other words, any two angles that look the same are the same. Also, when you add a Big angle to a Little angle, you get 180 degrees. That's pretty much all there is to know about parallel lines. You should be aware that parallelograms work the same way.

Any quadrilateral—a four-sided figure, like a square or rectangle—has 360 degrees. It doesn't matter if it looks like a box or a kite or the Star Trek insignia; as long as it has four sides, it has 360 degrees.

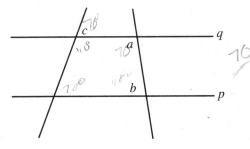

40. In the figure above, a quadrilateral is formed when the parallel lines p and q are cut by two transversals. If angle c is 70°, what is $a + b$?

   F.   70°
   G.   110°
   H.   140°
   J.   180°
   K.   It cannot be determined from the information given.

The way to deal with any geometry question is to go with what you know. Remember that there won't be any weird stuff and approach the questions with basic concepts in mind. In order to make questions hard, the test writers will combine different concepts in a single problem, but they'll never introduce things like calculus.

On any geometry question the first thing you want to do is label everything. In the problem, you're told that $\angle c$ is 70 degrees, so write that on the figure immediately. Because of the parallel lines, you also know seven other angles right away, so label the angles as well.

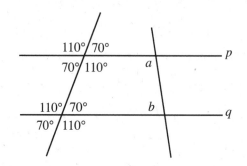

When the ACT offers you some version of "It cannot be determined," you're often dealing with a trap. Be very suspicious of this answer choice. It's almost never right (just the opposite of OMIT on the English test). Keep that in mind as you finish this question.

Don't pull your hair out trying to remember the intricacies of alternate interior angles; all you need to do is think about parallel lines more simply. In this question, what type of angles are *a* and *b*? One is Little and one is Big. What do we know about any Big angle and any Little angle? Their sum is 180°.

The answer is J.

All triangles all have 180 degrees. Always. Circles always have 360 degrees. Isosceles triangles have two sides that are equal, and the angles opposite those sides are also equal. With that in mind, let's take a look at the next problem:

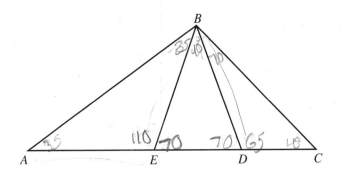

21. In the figure above, $\overline{AE} = \overline{BE} = \overline{BD}$ and

∠*EBD* = 40° and ∠*C* = 45°. What is the measure

of ∠*A*?

    A. 35°
    B. 40°
    C. 45°
    D. 70°
    E. 110°

As in the last question, the first thing we want to do is label the figure with all the information the question gives us. We're trying to get to ∠*A*, so let's try to work down in that direction.

Because the middle triangle is isosceles and its top angle is 40°, the other two angles must evenly split 140°. That means they're both 70°. Put that on your figure.

Because a straight line has 180°, we know that the angle next to 70° must be 110°. We're getting close now. The triangle on the left is also isosceles, so we can figure out the other two angles. Together, they add up to 70°, so each of them must be 35°. The correct answer is A.

Perimeter

The perimeter of an object is the lengths of its sides added together. For quadrilaterals, that's pretty straightforward. Add the four sides and there you go. For circles and triangles it can get a bit more interesting, but not much. Here are the two formulas you're going to need to know:

Circumference of a circle = $2\pi r$

Pythagorean theorem for right triangles = $a^2 + b^2 = c^2$

For the circumference (perimeter) of the circle, r is the radius. For the Pythagorean theorem, c is the side across from the right angle (the hypotenuse) and a and b are the other two sides (the legs).

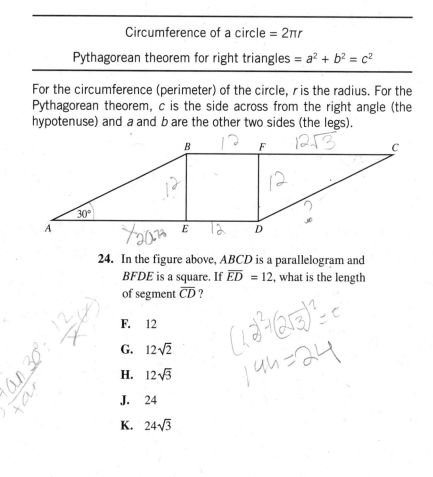

24. In the figure above, *ABCD* is a parallelogram and *BFDE* is a square. If $\overline{ED}$ = 12, what is the length of segment $\overline{CD}$?

F. 12

G. $12\sqrt{2}$

H. $12\sqrt{3}$

J. 24

K. $24\sqrt{3}$

After you label the figure with the information in the question, you can do some Ballparking. Use a piece of paper to make a ruler measuring 12 (the length of each side of the square). $\overline{CD}$ is clearly much more than 12. It's somewhere around double, so eliminate F and G.

$\overline{CD}$ is the hypotenuse of a right triangle, but we know only one of the sides. Fortunately, this is a special right triangle, with angles of 30°, 60°, and 90°. The sides of triangles like this are always in a fixed ratio of $1:\sqrt{3}:2$, respectively. Because the side we have is opposite the 30° angle, the sides in this triangle are in this ratio— $12:12\sqrt{3}:24$. So, $\overline{CD}$ = 24. Choice J is the correct answer.

Here's another perimeter problem for you to do:

> **51.** A regular hexagon is inscribed in a circle with circumference of 6π. What is the perimeter of the hexagon?
>
> **A.** 3
> **B.** 5.8π
> **C.** 9π
> **D.** 18
> **E.** There is insufficient information to answer the question.

Whenever ACT describes a figure but doesn't draw it for you, you should draw it yourself. It's much easier to do these problems if you have a visual reference. Sketch yourself a circle and then put a hexagon inside it. *Regular* means that all the sides and angles of the hexagon are the same. Don't worry about how pretty your figure looks—it's just to help you get the question right.

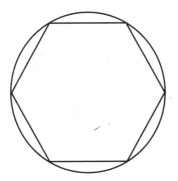

On circle questions, ACT nearly always asks about the radius, diameter, circumference, or area. If you know one of these four properties, you'll be able to find the others quickly. As a rule of thumb, it's a good idea to determine the radius before you start attacking a circle question, because you can obtain all other measurements from there. We're told that the circle has a circumference of 6π. Because we know the formula for a circle's circumference is $C = 2\pi r$, we can figure out the radius equals 3. If we put that on the figure, we'll see that the radius bisects the hexagon's angles and makes an equilateral triangle, so each side of the hexagon must be 3 also.

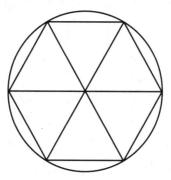

The perimeter of the hexagon is 18, choice D.

Area

Here are the main area formulas you'll need on the ACT. Remember that they aren't given to you at the beginning of the Math test, so you need to have them memorized.

Area Formulas for Basic Shapes

Square or Rectangle = $l \times w$

Circle = πr^2

Triangle = $\frac{1}{2}bh$

---

37. Sail cloth typically weighs 12 pounds per square yard. If it sells for $3.50 a pound, what is the cost of the cloth in a sail in the shape of a right triangle 30 feet tall and 15 feet wide at its base? (Note: There are 3 feet in a yard.)

A. $25.00
B. $87.50
C. $262.50
D. $1,050.00
E. $3,150.00

Question number 37 is a fairly involved area question. Before we find the area we'll need to convert feet to yards. Then we'll have to convert the area to pounds before finally calculating the cost of the cloth. The dimensions of 30 feet by 15 feet are the same as 10 yards by 5 yards. Now we can find the area using the formula for the area of a triangle.

$$\frac{1}{2}(10)(5) = 25$$

Now that we have the area, we can find the weight by multiplying by 12.
$$25 \times 12 = 300$$

Finally, get the cost.
$$300 \times \$3.50 = \$1,050.00$$

The answer is D.

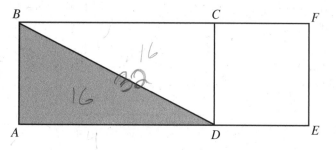

28. In the figure above, *ABCD* is a rectangle and *CDEF* is a square. If $\overline{DE} + \overline{EF} = \overline{AD}$ and the area of △*ABD* is 16, what is the area of rectangle *ABFE*?

   F.   16
   G.   32
   H.   36
   J.   48
   K. 288

The first thing to do here is ballpark and cross out K. It's far larger than is possible if the shaded triangle is only 16. Because the area of △*ABD* is 16, and it is half of the rectangle *ABCD*, the area of *ABCD* is 32. Because we'll have to add in the square *CDEF*, we can eliminate F, G, and H at this point. The only thing left is J. If you want to do this problem the real "math" way, drop us a line and we'll send you the explanation. Remember—the only important thing on the ACT is getting the right answer. How you get there is irrelevant.

Coordinate Geometry

You're expected to understand how graphing works before you walk into the test room. Fortunately, there's not much to it. In fact, you're allowed to bring a graphing calculator with you to use on the test (be sure your calculator is permissable—we've listed all banned calculators in Step 3: Ballparking in case you're not sure).

The critical bit of information (and just about the only thing people ever mix up) is that the x-axis goes left-right and the y-axis goes up-down. One way to keep that straight is to think about how you would write those letters—y goes up and down more than x does.

The folks who write the ACT want to make sure you know how to write an equation for a line. They also want you to know how to find the slope of a line. Okay. We can handle that. The first thing we'll address is how to find the slope of a line. If you have two points (x_1, y_1) and (x_2, y_2), use this formula:

$$\frac{y_1 - y_2}{x_1 - x_2} \text{ or } \frac{\text{rise}}{\text{run}}$$

It doesn't matter which point you use first, just keep the x and y parts in the same order on the top and the bottom.

The standard form for the equation of a line is

$$y = mx + b$$

In this form, m is the slope, and b is the y-intercept, which is just a fancy way of saying that the line crosses the y-axis at the point $(0, b)$.

There are two important things to remember about lines:

- Parallel lines have the same slope.

- The slopes of perpendicular lines are negative reciprocals of each other.

These bits of information cover the majority of slope questions. Figure out some way to remember them, because you're going to need them on the test. Don't forget about your graphing calculator. If you have the right programs, the calculator can be very useful on these questions.

27. Which of the following gives the equation of a line which intersects the y-axis at (0,–3) and is perpendicular to the line containing the points (2,–4) and (5,1)?

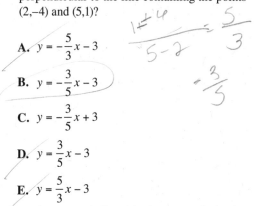

A. $y = -\dfrac{5}{3}x - 3$

B. $y = -\dfrac{3}{5}x - 3$

C. $y = -\dfrac{3}{5}x + 3$

D. $y = \dfrac{3}{5}x - 3$

E. $y = \dfrac{5}{3}x - 3$

Perpendicular lines have a relationship between their slopes (they're negative reciprocals), so that's a good place to start on this question. Let's figure out the slope for the first line. The negative reciprocal of that will be the slope of the second line.

Because we have points for the first line only, we have to use this formula to find its slope:

$$\frac{y_1 - y_2}{x_1 - x_2}$$

Remember that it doesn't matter which point you use first, but putting points with negative values second is easier because of the minus signs in the formula. So, that's what we'll do.

$$\frac{1 - (-4)}{5 - 2}$$

$\dfrac{5}{3}$ is the slope of the first line, so $-\dfrac{3}{5}$ is the slope of the line we're looking for. Right now you should eliminate A, D, and E, because they have other slopes.

The y-intercept was given in the question as –3, so that means the correct answer is B.

24. In the standard coordinate plane, the line formed by the equation $2x - y = 3$ passes through which of the following points?

   F. $(-1,1)$
   G. $(0,\frac{3}{2})$
   H. $(0,3)$
   J. $(1,-1)$
   K. $(2,3)$

Whenever you're asked which point fits a particular equation, the best thing you can do is PITA. Plug in those answers into the question and see which one works. In this kind of question, because the answers aren't in a strict numerical order, there's no point starting with the middle answer. Instead, start with answers that seem easier to calculate, like ones with 0 in them. Here's what happens for each of the answers when you use PITA.

   F. $(-1,1)$ $2(-1) - 1 = -2 - 1 = -3$ Not right.
   G. $(0,\frac{3}{2})$ $2(0) - \frac{3}{2} = -\frac{3}{2}$ Not right, either.
   H. $(0,3)$ $2(0) - 3 = -3$ Nope.
   J. $(1,-1)$ $2(1) - (-1) = 2 + 1 = 3$ Yes!
   K. $(2,3)$ $2(2) - 3 = 4 - 3 = 1$ Nope.

Choice J is the correct answer. You could also have graphed the line on your calculator and ballparked to find the point it passes through!

42. What is the distance between the points $(-2,4)$ and $(3,-3)$ on the standard coordinate plane?

   F. $\sqrt{12}$
   G. 12
   H. $\sqrt{74}$
   J. 74
   K. 144

You'll notice that we didn't teach you the distance formula earlier when discussing the important formulas for geometry. That's because it's unnecessary. When you see a question like this, the way to approach it is by sketching it. Connect the two points and then build a right triangle with them. The Pythagorean theorem will give you the distance between them (yes, we know that this is what the distance formula is based on).

Go ahead and try sketching the points and making the right triangle. You'll want to figure out how long each of the legs is, too. Write the lengths onto the triangle. After you've done that (and only after you've done that), go ahead and take a look at the drawing we did. It's no good looking ahead—you'll get better at this stuff only if you do it yourself, so get sketching.

Are you done? Okay, here's our sketch:

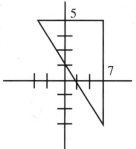

Your sketch should be pretty much like this one. It's okay if you made the triangle under the two points instead of above them, as we did. It works both ways. Now that you've got the right triangle and the lengths of the legs, you can figure out the distance between the points.

$5^2 + 7^2 = $ distance^2

$25 + 49 = $ distance^2

$\sqrt{74} = $ distance^2

So, H is the correct answer.

Trig!

There are only four trigonometry questions on the ACT. That means, if you hate trig, you could stop here, go on to the Reading test, and probably never see much of a difference. However, we think you should stick with us for a couple more pages because two of those four trig questions are always based on the way simple trig functions are related to a right triangle. Understanding how to do them doesn't take long and guarantees you two more raw points on your Math test. So here we go.

SOHCAHTOA

The trig functions sine, cosine, and tangent can all be calculated by using a right triangle. Here's a triangle that we will use to show you how.

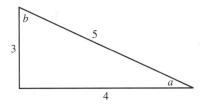

All of the functions can be calculated using the lengths of the sides of the triangle. Here's how:

$$\sin = \frac{\text{opposite}}{\text{hypotenuse}} \qquad \cos = \frac{\text{adjacent}}{\text{hypotenuse}} \qquad \tan = \frac{\text{opposite}}{\text{adjacent}}$$

If you look at the first letter of each word [(S)in equals (O)pposite over (H)ypotenuse, etc.], you'll see that it spells out the name of this section of the book: SOHCAHTOA. This will help you remember how each function is calculated. We'll show you how on the triangle above.

Suppose we wanted to find sin(*a*). Sine is opposite over hypotenuse, so we need to find those two sides' values. The side opposite *a* is 3, and the hypotenuse is 5, so here's how sine of *a* would look:

$$\sin(a) = \frac{3}{5}$$

Cos(*a*) is found in a similar way. Because cosine is adjacent over hypotenuse, we need those two sides.

$$\cos(a) = \frac{\text{adjacent}}{\text{hypotenuse}} \text{ which becomes } \cos(a) = \frac{4}{5}.$$

Use SOHCAHTOA to figure out sin(*b*), cos(*b*), and tan(*b*). The answers are at the end of this chapter.

As we said, you can use SOHCAHTOA to do two of the four trig questions on just about every ACT we've ever seen (the other two questions deal with things such as trig graphing, which are beyond the scope of this book). Here's how it would work on what may seem to be an impossible problem at first. Watch carefully, because ACT loves this kind of problem.

514 feet

54. Ijiru is inside the St. Louis Arch, looking out one of the observation windows located 514 feet above the ground. He is looking downward at a 52° angle from a point directly below the window at a fountain. Which of the following correctly gives the distance from the arch to the fountain if that distance is represented by *x*?

F. 514 cos52° = *x*

G. 514 sin52° = *x*

H. 514 tan52° = *x*

J. $\dfrac{\sin 52°}{514} = x$

K. $\dfrac{\tan 52°}{514} = x$

Remember that we said trig questions are frequently based on the right triangle relationships of the trig functions? Well, that's what's going on in this question. The first thing you need to do is sketch in a right triangle and label the angle and any information you know, like the height of the arch, like this:

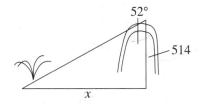

Now that you've done that, you're almost done. The key to success is figuring out which trig function to use. This is where SOHCAHTOA comes in handy. The angle we'll use is given—it's the angle at the top of the arch. The sides we'll use are given as well—the height of the arch (the side adjacent to the angle) and the distance from the bottom of the arch to the fountain (the side opposite from the angle). Because we're using the sides opposite and adjacent, only one trig function could possibly work—tangent. Tangent is opposite over adjacent, so we can put it all together like this:

$$\tan 52° = \frac{x}{514}$$

With just a little manipulation, this becomes

$$514 \tan 52° = x$$

The answer is H. That wasn't so bad now, was it?

Answers to quiz in SOHCAHTOA section:

$$\sin(b) = \frac{3}{5}, \cos(b) = \frac{4}{5}, \tan(b) = \frac{4}{3}$$

Step 7:
Follow the
Four Steps

Reading: Don't Do It!

The Reading test of the ACT is the most poorly named section of the test. When most people sit down to do the Reading test, they start by reading the passage. That's exactly what the test writers expect you will do, and it's exactly what they want you to do because it wastes your time.

Reading passages on the ACT are long; they average around 85–90 lines. There's no way that the average test taker (that's you) can thoroughly read all four passages and still have time to do all 40 questions on the test. It just won't work. You need a different approach.

Before we get into exactly how you are going to do the reading, let's review what's on the Reading test.

Four Tests, Forty Questions

The Reading test always has four passages, each with ten questions. The passages always have short blurbs that provide author and title, and they always appear in this order: prose fiction, social science, humanities, and natural science. The questions have four answer choices each and are in no particular order of difficulty. As we already noted, the passages are usually around 85–90 lines long.

What to Do, What to Do

The key to your success on the Reading test is taking control of the test. Most students take the test in the order in which it is given. They do the prose fiction passage first, then the social science, then the humanities, and then, if they have any time left, the natural science passage. This is unwise.

It's unwise because how well you do on a reading passage depends in part on how much you like the topic you are reading about. Boring topics are harder to do because, well, they're boring. You daydream. Topics that interest you are easier to do because you pay more attention to them. You're engrossed.

How do you know which passages will be interesting to you and which will be boring before you start the test? You don't. That's why you must spend the first minute of the Reading test flipping through and looking at the passages.

When you come back from the break and the proctor tells you to begin test three (also known as Reading), the first thing you should do is read the blurb for each passage and decide where you're going to begin. If you're lucky, you'll find a passage that interests you somewhat and you can start there. Or maybe you'll find a passage that you know you'll hate, and you can plan to do that one last.

If you discover that all four passages are equally annoying, you should start with the type of passage on which you usually do best. For some people, that's natural science. For others, it's prose fiction. It doesn't matter which you like best; what matters is that you reorder the passages to take advantage of your strengths.

So Many Passages, So Little Time

For many of us the prospect of completing all four reading passages in the time allotted is pretty intimidating. But we all know that you have to finish a test to get a good score, right? Well, in *school* that's true, but the ACT *isn't* school. You can get a good score without finishing the test. In fact, time pressure is one of the things that the ACT deliberately uses against you, so you need to know what to do to get the score you're shooting for.

What if you needed to do only three passages in the 35 minutes they give you for the Reading test? Would that be better? Could you get a higher percentage of the questions you complete correct if you didn't have to push through to that fourth passage? Of course you could. And you could get a pretty decent score, too. The key, though, is accuracy.

On the Reading test the answers are right there in the passages. Given enough time, you should be able to find them. Your accuracy would be pretty high if you had unlimited time. We can't get you that, but by skipping one passage you'll get a lot more time per passage, and that's a good start. If you can complete three of the four passages with 80 percent accuracy (getting eight right out of every ten questions, or 24 right for the set of 30) and then guess on the ten questions you skip from the fourth passage, you'll get about 26 raw points. That generally works out to a 25 on the Reading test, which is the 81st percentile.

That's not too shabby. If you're getting a 23 or lower on the Reading test right now, you should try this method the next time you take a practice test, and make sure you have the feel for how to slow down enough to improve your accuracy. Improve it enough to where you're missing only one question per passage, and you'll get a 27 on the Reading test. That's the 90th percentile—*without* doing a whole passage.

Keep in mind, too, that some questions are easier than others. When five minutes remain in the section, you should make sure the last questions you do are easy ones. How can you tell? Look for short questions, line numbers in the question, and lots of proper nouns in the question or answers (easier to find when you're scanning the passage for the answer).

I've Picked a Passage. Now What?

Once you decide on an order for your passages, you'll do them, one by one, in the same way. You'll ignore the passage entirely and go right to the questions. If you're great at skimming, though, it's okay to skim the passage quickly before going to the questions, but spend no more than 45 seconds skimming.

You want to get to the questions as fast as you can because that's where all the points are. There are no points awarded for time spent reading the passage. All the points on the Reading test are handed out for one thing and one thing only: correctly answering the questions.

Now you may be thinking that the only way to do the questions is to read the passage. The questions are based on the content of the passage, right? Correct. But what you're overlooking is the fact that the majority of each reading passage is not even asked about in the questions. ACT tends to ask about the same parts of the passage and, because the passage is so long (85–90 lines!), the entire passage is rarely used in creating the questions.

You do have to read to get the questions right, but you should read ONLY what you need to get the questions right. Your job is to learn how to focus your reading to do the questions while ignoring the rest of the passage.

Questions First

Just as you reordered the passages to take advantage of your strengths, you are also going to reorder the questions in each passage to take advantage of their weaknesses. All reading questions are not created equal. There are a number of different types, and some of them are definitely harder than others. We're going to explain some of them to you and walk you through an example of each before turning you loose to do some on your own in the practice section of this book. All of the questions we do in this chapter will be based on the passage on the next page.

Remember: Don't read it just yet. It's been formatted so that you can remove it from the book and keep it available for each question you do, so go get a pair of scissors, cut the passage out of the book, and set it aside. Don't toss it out when you're done with this chapter, either—there are seven more questions based on it in the practice section.

HUMANITIES: This passage is adapted from The Great Depression by T. H. Watkins. Copyright ©1993 Blackside, Inc. By permission of Little, Brown and Company (Inc). In it, Watkins discusses the World's Fairs staged in the United States during the Great Depression.

One of the peculiarities of the years of the Great Depression was the fact that in the middle of the worst economic period Americans had ever seen, four cities somehow found the time, money, and energy to produce four World's Fairs—more than during any other ten-year period in the nation's history. The first, Chicago's "Century of Progress" celebration, opened
5 for business on a 400-acre landfill on the edge of Lake Michigan on April 29, 1933. The fair, said its president, Rufus C. Dawes, on opening day, was "the spontaneous expression of the pride of citizenship of Chicago" and, furthermore, demonstrated man's "power to prevail over the perils that beset him." Over the two years of the fair's life, 38 million people came to witness its attractions, giving the city of Chicago a helpful shot of income for several months
10 (although the fair itself lost money, as World's Fairs tend to do).

Hoping to duplicate Chicago's economy-boosting success, on June 6, 1936, Texans celebrated the hundredth anniversary of their independence from Mexico by producing the Texas Centennial Exposition in Dallas and a smaller, though related, Frontier Centennial Exposition in Fort Worth. Before closing down in December, the combined expositions drew some
15 7 million visitors, and if that appeared insignificant when compared to the Chicago fair, the celebration accomplished its principal task, according to Stanley Marcus, cofounder of the mercantile empire of Neiman-Marcus. "I've frequently said that modern Texas history started with the celebration of the Texas Centennial," he remembered, "because it was in 1936 . . . that the rest of America discovered Texas."

20 Then there were the two great fairs that marked the end of the decade—San Francisco's Golden Gate Exposition, which opened on February 18, 1939, and the New York World's Fair, which opened on April 30, 1939; both ran until the fall of 1940. Neither brought in anywhere near the number of people Chicago's fair had in 1933, but each stood at the cusp between two historical epochs and consequently would shine forth more brilliantly in the
25 national memory, both burdened and enhanced by their roles as symbols.

San Francisco's exposition was designed to celebrate the completion of the Oakland–San Francisco Bay Bridge and the Golden Gate Bridge across the entrance to the San Francisco Bay, two of the certifiably triumphant engineering accomplishments of the age. The fair itself was distinguished particularly by the fact that it was erected on a 400-acre landfill.

30 There was a Westinghouse robot and "Pedro the Vodor," a keyboard-operated talking machine invented by the Bell Telephone Laboratories. Another well-publicized distinction of the fair was the presence of nude fan dancer Sally Rand, who had debuted at the Chicago Fair; her show had now expanded to include a "nude ranch" populated by 47 showgirls who pitched horseshoes, rode burros, and did other ranch-like activities dressed mainly in ten-gallon hats,
35 cowboy boots, and G-strings.

The inspiration for the New York World's Fair, built 5 miles from downtown Manhattan on a 1,200-acre Long Island refuse site called the Corona Dump, was the inauguration of President George Washington 150 years before, which the fair's leaders chose to identify as the true moment when the United States of America opened for business. The theme of
40 the fair was "The World of Tomorrow," and it featured the definitive futuristic symbols of the age: a 750-foot-high spike called the Trylon and, by its side, an enormous globe called the Perisphere, 200 feet in diameter. (Devotees of the Golden Gate Exposition, it was said, criticized these symbols as being faintly suggestive.) The fair was crawling with its own forward-looking exhibits—a robot named Elektro, a simulated trip to the moon, and the first
45 public demonstration of television, among others—but the most ambitious was "Futurama," a $7.5 million exhibit funded by General Motors and designed by Norman Bel Geddes. With 500,000 miniature buildings, a million little trees, and 50,000 tiny automobiles that ran like beetles over complex highway networks, the huge exhibit pictured what Bel Geddes thought America would be like in the year 1960.

50 If the great industrial designer's vision of the future was not entirely reliable (he predicted that his teardrop-shaped automobiles would cost only $200, for one thing), it was no more flawed than the vision of the current world that both the Golden Gate Exhibition and the New York World's Fair presented. The ornate mix of Mayan, Cambodian, Burmese, Malayan, and Polynesian architectural styles that characterized most of the buildings on San Francis-
55 co's Treasure Island, for example, was called "Pacific Basin," and the fair's busy publicity machine repeatedly emphasized the wonderful unity of prosperity and cooperation that the peoples of the Pacific Rim nations enjoyed and presumably would continue to enjoy. For its part, the New York fair's own publicity people touted the beauty and hope represented by its Lagoon of Nations, its Hall of Nations, and its Court of Peace bordered by the flags
60 of the 58 foreign countries that had chosen to participate in the fair, 21 of which had erected their own buildings or pavilions, including Italy, the USSR, France, Great Britain, Japan, and Belgium. So had the League of Nations, that engine of universal peace that had been established (without the participation of the United States) after the first World War.

The Big Technique: Follow the Four Steps

Success on the Reading test is the result of a focused approach. The questions are written to mislead you, and the wrong answers are there to confuse you; the test writers are great at this. This is because most people read the passage, read a question, and then read the answer choices for that question. Then they mull the choices over before finally picking one. Occasionally they'll refer back to the passage, but not usually. This is a terrible approach. You are smarter. You will follow these Four Steps.

Step 1—Read the Question

When you read the question, put it into your own words before going to the passage to find the answer.

Step 2—Find the Answer into the Passage

Use the line reference or lead word (explained later in this chapter) to locate the part of the passage with the answer in it. Read there until you've figured out the answer.

Step 3—Put the Answer into Your Own Words

This is the most important step. You must put the answer into your own words before you go back to look at the answer choices. You do this to confirm that you really understand what you're reading and to avoid falling for any of the traps that are waiting in the wrong answer choices.

Step 4—POE

Read the answers and cross off any that don't agree with your answer.

Line Reference

You should always do questions that include line numbers or paragraph numbers first. You'll have to do some reading for every question on the test, but if you start with these line reference questions, you won't be shooting in the dark. These types of questions tell you where to look for the answer. Always remember to put the question into your own words before going to the passage and to put the answer into your own words before coming back to the answer choices.

Let's do this question using the Four Steps:

> 1. The theme presented by the Chicago "Century of Progress" celebration in line 4 was that:
>   A. humankind can triumph over adversity.
>   B. the Depression was almost over.
>   C. the future held world peace.
>   D. prosperous times were ahead for all Americans.

This question tells you that the information you need is in line 4. Never read only the indicated lines. Start about five lines earlier and continue about five lines past, adjusting for where sentences begin and end.

The first thing you should do is put the question into your own words. You should have something like, "What was the theme of the Chicago celebration?" Then go to the passage.

Start at line 4 with "The first," and read until the end of the paragraph. Well, what was the theme of the celebration? Put it into your own words before going to the answers. You should have something similar to "The people of Chicago are proud, and mankind can make it through hard times." If that's not what you thought it was saying, you should reread the passage now.

Now compare your answer to the answer choices. None of them mentions Chicago, but A sounds like what we got from the passage. Choice B mentions the Depression, which isn't discussed here. Choices C and D also talk about stuff that just isn't mentioned in this part of the passage. The correct answer is A.

Lead Word Questions

Unfortunately, many questions do not include line numbers. The problem you face then is figuring out which part of the passage to read. No problem. You are going to pick out words in the question that jump out at you—lead words—and use them to help you find where to read in the passage.

It's a bit like looking something up in the dictionary. If you're looking for the definition of "peripatetic," you wouldn't start at A and read every entry until you finally reached the one you want. No, you'd flip to the P's and start scanning for "peripatetic" until you found it. That's how lead words work. You scan the passage until you find them and then start reading to find the answer.

Try it out on this question:

> **2.** According to the passage, Norman Bel
> Geddes was:

There are no line numbers here, but there are great lead words. Names make for great lead words because they are capitalized. That makes them jump out of the passage when you scan it. Scan the passage now for Norman Bel Geddes, and read until you figure out what the passage says he was.

He shows up in lines 46–49. Reading from five lines before there to five lines after the end of that paragraph tells you that he designed "Futurama" (long before Matt Groening came on the scene) and that he was a great industrial designer (although he was wrong about the future). Great. On to the answer choices:

> **F.** an inventor.
> **G.** an industrial designer.
> **H.** a clairvoyant.
> **J.** an economist.

Clearly, G is supported by the passage and is correct. Good job.

Reverse Lead Word

Sometimes, the question doesn't have any great lead words, but the answer choices do. This frequently happens when you're being asked to identify a particular place or person. No big deal. Use the answer choices as your lead words. Consider this question:

> **3.** World's Fairs were held in all of the following states in the Great Depression EXCEPT:
>
> **A.** Illinois.
> **B.** Texas.
> **C.** Florida.
> **D.** California.

This question is not only a reverse lead word question, it's an EXCEPT question. Generally, you want to save EXCEPT questions for last because they involve finding three "correct" answers and one "incorrect" answer—much more work. Nevertheless, we're going to tackle this one.

Because the question doesn't have a great lead word ("Great Depression" doesn't count because the entire passage is about the Great Depression), let's look at the answer choices. Place names are easy to find because they are capitalized, so these should work well. Read the question, put it into your own words, and then start scanning the passage for the answer choices.

Chicago comes up almost immediately, and because that's in Illinois, you can cross out A. Remember, on an EXCEPT question you're looking for the "wrong" answer. *Texans* pops up pretty quickly in line 11, and Texas in line 13, so answer B is gone, too. Line 20 mentions San Francisco as a fair site, so there goes D. The correct answer is C. POE wins again.

Step 8:
Digging for Data

Science

The Science test is always the last multiple-choice part of the ACT. It is 35 minutes long and contains 40 questions. There are seven passages in this section: three charts and graphs passages, three experiments passages, and one "fighting scientists" passage. This chapter will deal primarily with charts and graphs. The most important thing for you to remember when facing the Science test is this: You don't need to know any science to do the ACT Science test.

Sounds strange, we know. Why call a test a science test if no scientific knowledge is required? Still, the fact remains that you don't need to know science to do the science. Here's why.

The ACT is a nationally administered test that is intended to be fair to all test takers (we won't get into the question of what makes a test fair here; we'll just accept that as the intention). In order for it to be fair, all the questions must be equally difficult (or easy) for all test takers.

If the Science test were to focus on a particular area of scientific knowledge, the test would immediately lose any fairness in that area because different high schools have different science curricula. Students lucky enough to attend schools that covered what was on the ACT would do better on the test. Students from schools that focused their science programs on other areas would suffer on the test.

So to avoid this sort of bias on the test, all the information needed to do each and every question is provided in the corresponding passage. You will not need to bring any outside scientific knowledge to the test. Everything you need will be right there on the page in front of you.

The science passages are never in any particular order. You'll have the right total number of charts and graphs, experiments, and fighting scientists passages, but they usually come all in a jumble. There's also no order of difficulty. The final passages on a section are frequently pretty simple, with a tricky passage somewhere in the middle eating up students' time. So, just as you did on the Reading test, you'll need to reorder the passages on the Science test. If you're doing a passage and it seems too tricky, move on to the next one. You can always come back to it later. If you do well on experiments passages, skip around the test and do all three experiments passages before trying any of the other passages. Don't feel obligated to do the passages in the order they are given to you.

Junk

Because the science passages don't require scientific knowledge, doing many of the questions becomes largely a matter of looking up information and drawing conclusions about the data presented. With questions like these, the test writers are forced to find some way to make the test difficult, and what they've chosen to do is fill the passages with junk in hopes of distracting you and wasting your time.

The Big Technique: Ignore the Intro

With the exception of the fighting scientists passage, every science passage has a generous amount of useless and often confusing information in it. This extra information is usually presented in the introduction to the passage. In these introductions, the test writers will give lengthy and complex explanations of the science on which the passage is based. Rarely will any questions refer to these explanations, however. So why are they there? To intimidate you and slow you down.

Most test takers expect the information on a test to be useful or at least important, so when they are taking a test, they read what is presented and attempt to understand it before going to the questions. That's what the test writers expect you to do, and that's what you must not do. As with the Reading test, all the points are given for doing questions, not reading stuff. And because most of the questions involve looking up information in the charts and tables—not referring back to the introduction—reading the introduction at all is a waste of your time. What's worse is that the introductions are frequently quite confusing, and reading them can frustrate you, which is never how you want to take a test.

For every science passage you do, with the exception of fighting scientists passages (which we'll discuss in Step 9), skip the introduction and go directly to the rest of the passage. For charts and graphs passages, that will mean looking at the charts, and for experiments passages, that will mean looking at the experiments (we'll deal with experiments passages in greater detail in Step 9 as well).

Note: If you come to a question that seems unrelated to the charts and experiments, then you should look at the intro, but not before that.

The Questions

There are three types of questions on the Science test (except with the fighting scientists passage, which is a separate issue altogether). We call these types of questions: Look it up, What if? and Why?

- **Look it up** questions are the easiest types of questions to do. They ask you to look up a specific piece of information in one of the charts or tables. Sometimes you'll be looking up multiple pieces of information and comparing them.

- **What if?** questions ask you to make predictions, draw conclusions, and analyze data. Don't get worried about this, though. The predictions are extensions of the data you're already given with no tricks thrown in. If something is getting hotter as time goes by and you're asked to predict its temperature after some more time passes, usually only one of the answer choices will give a higher temperature. What is being tested is your ability to look at the data and figure out how it is changing.

- **Why?** questions tend to be the trickiest. They deal with the ideas behind how experiments are set up and how the scientific process works. You might be asked to identify a control, explain an assumption, or determine the best way to study a particular variable.

Charts and Graphs

There are three charts and graphs passages on the Science test. Each one of them has five questions. These passages usually have one or two graphs or tables on which the majority of the questions are based.

There is generally a preponderance of Look it up questions for these passages. The charts and graphs passages have introductions, which you should ignore.

The first thing you want to do is take a look at the charts or tables. Read only enough of them to determine what is being represented. This usually means reading the labels on the sides and any labels that are on the graphs themselves. As soon as you're done with that, go directly to the questions.

The method for answering the questions is not as involved as that for the Reading test. In the Science test, the questions will typically tell you exactly where to go to find the information you need and what to do when you get there. The majority of the questions are testing your ability to look up data and draw conclusions about it, so if you're careful in doing that, you should be able to do well. The thing to keep in mind is that everything you need in order to answer the questions is given to you. You don't need to know how atomic decay works to do a passage about atomic decay; you just need to know how to read. Everything you need is provided, so relax! Let's do a passage now, keeping all of this in mind.

Newton's law of universal gravitation says that any two bodies attract each other according to a force that varies inversely as the square of the distance between them. Thus, when scientists try to launch a rocket (or any such projectile) into space, they must make sure that the rocket has enough energy to overcome the gravitational force on it due to the planet below. The minimum velocity necessary to be able to escape the planet's gravity is called the *escape velocity*. Escape velocity depends only on the radius and mass of a given planet; the mass of the projectile is irrelevant. Table 1 lists some escape velocities, masses, and radii of different planets and other celestial bodies.

Table 1			
Celestial Body	Mass (x 10^{24} kg)	Radius (x 10^6 m)	Escape Velocity (km/s)
Mercury	0.32	2.4	4.3
Venus	4.9	6.1	10.3
Earth	6	6.4	11.2
Mars	0.64	3.4	5
Jupiter	1900	70	60
Saturn	570	58	36
Uranus	87	23	22
Neptune	103	22	24
Pluto	0.0014	1.5	1.1
Moon	0.0074	1.7	2.3
Sun	1,991,000	700	618

Remember: You don't want to read the introductions for science passages unless you're doing a fighting scientists passage. This is a charts and graphs passage, so you should have skipped the intro. The first thing you should have done was look at the table. After seeing that it lists mass, radius, and escape velocity for a bunch of planets, you should have been done with that and ready to go on to the questions.

1. The scientists conclude that as the radius of a body increases, so does the escape velocity. Which of the following pairs of bodies does NOT support this conclusion?

   A. Mars and Earth
   B. Mercury and Jupiter
   C. Venus and the Moon
   D. Uranus and Neptune

This question wants you to find a pair of bodies for which the escape velocity and radius do not have a direct relationship. Be very careful on these NOT questions to keep track of exactly what they are looking for. To do this, then, you need to look at how escape velocity changes as radius increases for each pair of bodies.

When you look at the chart, one thing you should notice is that there are no obvious trends in the data. Sometimes everything in one column is increasing as everything in another column is decreasing. When that happens, note it. It's not the case here, though.

The radius of Earth is greater than the radius of Mars, but the escape velocity of Earth is also greater than the escape velocity of Mars, so this supports the conclusion. Because we want something that doesn't support the conclusion, cross out choice A. The radius of Jupiter is greater than the radius of Mercury, but Jupiter's escape velocity is greater than that of Mercury, so B is out, too. The radius of Venus is greater than the radius of the Moon, but Venus's escape velocity is greater than that of the Moon, so C is gone as well. That leaves D. The radius of Uranus is greater than the radius of Neptune, but the escape velocity for Uranus is less than the escape velocity for Neptune, so this doesn't support the conclusion. Choice D is the correct answer.

2. A rocket of mass 5,000 kg is launched from the surfaces of different bodies at a velocity of 4.8 km/s. From which of the following planets would the rocket NOT be able to escape?

   F. Mercury
   G. Mars
   H. the Moon
   J. Pluto

This is another NOT question. Here, they give us an escape velocity and ask for which body this escape velocity would not be high enough to get the rocket out into space. All you need to do, then, is check the bodies given in the answer choices and see which one has an escape velocity higher than 4.8 km/s. It's Mars, so the answer is G.

3. Based on the data in the table, which of the following best explains why the Sun's escape velocity is very large?

    A. The surface temperature of the Sun is much greater than that of any of the other bodies listed.
    B. The Sun is the only body listed that does not orbit.
    C. The Sun has both a large mass and a large radius.
    D. The Sun will eventually collapse, causing a black hole to form. Because nothing can escape a black hole, the Sun must have a very large escape velocity.

This is a Why? question. You need to prove that you understand something about the information presented. This is an example of a question for which you'll have to go back to the introduction to find the answer. What does the introduction say about what makes an escape velocity large or small? "Escape velocity depends only on the radius and mass of a given planet." Let's look at the answer choices.

Choice A is true but has nothing to do with escape velocity, according to the passage. Choice B is also irrelevant. Choice C sounds like what the passage said, and D is just ridiculous, so C is correct, because it's the only choice that could be supported by the information in the table.

4. The scientists predict that the escape velocity of a planet also depends on the planet's distance from the Sun. Which of the following best refutes this hypothesis?

    F. A planet's distance from the Sun changes as it orbits, but the escape velocity never does.
    G. As a planet's mass increases, so does its escape velocity.
    H. As a planet's radius decreases, its escape velocity increases.
    J. Planets far away from the Sun tend to be much colder than planets close to the Sun.

Here's another Why? question. This one wants you to contradict a hypothesis. The best way to do that is to disagree with it directly. The hypothesis is that escape velocity is related to distance from the Sun. Look for an answer that says this isn't so. Choice F looks attractive—distance changes but escape velocity doesn't. That's pretty much the direct opposite of the hypothesis, so F is probably correct, but we should check the other answer choices. Choice G doesn't address distance from the Sun, so it can't be refuting the hypothesis. Same for H. Choice J discusses distance from the Sun, but only how it relates to the temperature of a planet, not its escape velocity. Choice F is correct.

5. Scientists discover a tenth planet beyond Pluto, which they call Rupert. The escape velocity of a 1,000 kg rocket on Rupert is 4.0 km/s. What would the escape velocity for a 2,000 kg rocket be on Rupert?

   A. 2.0 km/s
   B. 4.0 km/s
   C. 8.0 km/s
   D. 16.0 km/s

This question is about escape velocity as it relates to a rocket's mass. The table doesn't list any information about the mass of a rocket and how it affects escape velocity, so it probably has no effect, but let's check the introduction just to be sure. Sure enough, at the end of the intro it says, "the mass of the projectile is irrelevant." So the escape velocity will be the same regardless of the mass of the rocket. The answer is B.

Step 9:
Comparing and
Contrasting

Experiments

There are three experiments passages in every Science test. Each one has six questions, and they usually have graphs or tables for you to work with. The structure of an experiments passage is always the same. An experiment is conducted and results are given to you. Then, some aspect of the experiment is changed—maybe the temperature, maybe the weight of something—and the experiment is repeated and the results are given to you again. Usually, something else is changed and the experiment is run a third time; then it's on to the questions. Sometimes, though, there is a fourth experiment. That's nothing to worry about; the pattern of experiment-change-experiment is always followed.

The key to the questions in the experiments passages is knowing which experiments they refer to. The types of questions are the same as those described in the previous chapter, so you'll use the same techniques. All you need to add to the mix is determining which experiment to refer to when doing each question. Because each experiment is essentially the same as the first one with only a slight change, focusing on those changes is going to be your mission in the experiments passages.

The Big Technique: Spot the Difference

To do the questions quickly, you need to know where to find the information they require. To do that, you need to know what is going on in each experiment. As with most science passages, you'll ignore the introduction on the experiments passages, but you will need to read the description of each of the three (or four) experiments.

When you're reading the descriptions of the experiments, you need to decide what makes each one different and note that next to the experiment. Sometimes, you won't write anything at all next to the first one; the other experiments are the "different" experiments. Your notes should be just that—notes. Don't write a whole bunch of stuff. If the second experiment is a repeat of the first, but with different sizes for everything, just write "diff. sizes" next to it and go on. You still get points only for doing the questions, so you don't want to spend too much time on the reading.

Read these three experiments and write down how each one is different.

Experiment 1

Here, a bar 0.5 m long was rotated at different angular velocities through a magnetic field of strength 10 Tesla. The scientists obtained the following data:

Angular Velocity (rad/s)	Potential Difference (Volts)
10	12.5
15	18.8
20	25.0
25	31.3
30	37.6

Experiment 2

The scientists now rotated various iron bars through a 30 T magnetic field at an angular velocity of 40 rad/sec.

Length of bar (m)	Potential Difference (Volts)
0.25	37.5
0.50	150.0
0.75	337.5
1.00	600.0

Experiment 3

Now, the scientists used a bar 0.75 m long rotating at an angular velocity of 20 rad/s while varying the magnetic field strength.

Magnetic Field Strength (Tesla)	Potential Difference (Volts)
10	56.25
20	112.50
30	168.75
40	225.00
50	281.25

In this example it's fine to have written something by the first experiment. You could have written "diff. vel." by the first experiment, "diff. length" by the second, and "diff. mag. field" by the third. Anything similar to this would be fine. If you wrote more than three or four words, you're probably overthinking things. If you didn't write anything, you should have. Our techniques work only if you practice them on paper, not just in your head. No one ever became a great guitarist by simply reading about guitar technique, and the same goes for the ACT.

Once you've read the experiments and determined how they differ, it's time to head for the questions. Approach them just as you did the charts and graphs questions in the last chapter (if you haven't read Step 8 yet, go back and do so now before continuing here).

Here's the entire passage for you:

> It is a well-known fact that charged particles moving through a magnetic field will feel a force that depends on their charge, their velocity, and the strength of the magnetic field. Thus, when a conductor moves through a magnetic field, it will become polarized and an electric field will form inside it. In particular, if a metal rod rotates at constant

angular velocity through a magnetic field perpendicular to the plane of the bar (see figure below), the two ends of the bar will have a difference in electric potential between them. In the experiments below, scientists used iron bars rotating at constant angular velocities and measured the difference in potential between the two ends.

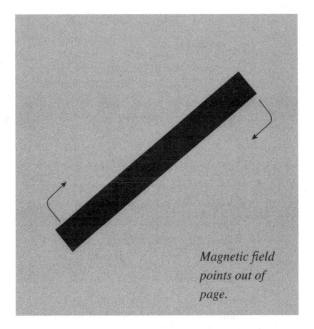

Magnetic field points out of page.

Experiment 1

Here, a bar 0.5 m long was rotated at different angular velocities through a magnetic field of strength 10 Tesla. The scientists obtained the following data:

Angular Velocity (rad/s)	Potential Difference (Volts)
10	12.5
15	18.8
20	25.0
25	31.3
30	37.6

Experiment 2

The scientists now rotated various iron bars through a 30 T magnetic field at an angular velocity of 40 rad/s.

Length of bar (m)	Potential Difference (Volts)
0.25	37.5
0.50	150.0
0.75	337.5
1.00	600.0

Experiment 3

Now, the scientists used a bar 0.75 m long rotating at an angular velocity of 20 rad/s while varying the magnetic field strength.

Magentic Field Strength (Tesla)	Potential Difference (Volts)
10	56.25
20	112.5
30	168.75
40	225.00
50	281.25

Copy the notes you made earlier in the chapter to the experiments above, and then go on to the questions. Remember to use the techniques we taught you in the last chapter.

Did you notice that there are clear trends in the data? In each table as one value increases, the other *also* increases. That's not something you want to overlook.

1. Which of the following hypotheses was tested in experiment 2?

   A. Magnetic field strength is directly related to potential difference.
   B. Length is directly related to angular velocity.
   C. Angular velocity is directly related to potential difference.
   D. Potential difference is directly related to length.

A question about the hypothesis is really asking, "What did the scientists mess around with and what did they measure?" Anything that was held constant cannot be what was being studied because, on the ACT, the only way to study something is to fool around with it. So what did they mess with in experiment 2? They changed the length of the bar. Eliminate A and C because they don't mention length. What was being measured? Potential difference—the correct answer is D.

2. According to the data taken, one way to increase the potential difference between the two ends of a given bar rotating in a magnetic field would be to:

   F. use steel bars instead of iron ones.
   G. decrease the strength of the magnetic field.
   H. decrease the length of the bar.
   J. increase the bar's angular velocity.

Right away, you should cross off F. It's ridiculous and has nothing to do with what was mentioned in the experiments. The question wants you to increase potential difference, so check out what made that happen in the experiments. In experiment 1, increased angular velocity resulted in increased potential difference. Hey! That's what J says! Choice J is probably right, but check the other experiments. In experiment 2, increased length resulted in increased potential difference. That's the opposite of H, so cross H out. In experiment 3, increased field strength resulted in increased potential difference. That's the opposite of G, so G is out. Choice J is correct.

3. A bar 0.75 m long rotates with an angular velocity of 20 rad/s in a magnetic field of magnitude 100 T. The potential difference of the bar is most nearly:

A. 125 volts.
B. 281.25 volts.
C. 563 volts.
D. 1,000 volts.

This question is asking you to make a prediction based on trends in data you already have. So, find the appropriate experiment and determine where this hypothetical bar would fall. A bar 0.75 m long with an angular velocity of 20 rad/s fits in with experiment 3. A field of 100 T is double the highest value listed. How does potential difference change as field strength doubles? The table says the potential difference is 56.26 at 10 T and 112.50 at 20 T, so it doubles as the field strength doubles. The answer we want, then, is double the field strength at 50 T. So, double 281.25 and you get 562.5, or C.

4. The data indicates that when the magnetic field strength doubles, the potential difference:

F. quadruples.
G. doubles.
H. remains the same.
J. halves.

Heh, heh, heh. We already dealt with this in question number 3. It's great when this happens on the test (and it happens a lot). The answer is G.

5. As the potential difference between the two ends
of a given bar increases, the time it takes for a
charged particle to move from one end to the
other decreases. For a bar 0.5 m long rotating
at 40 rad/s, which of the following magnetic
fields would make the time it takes for a charged
particle to move from one end to the other the
largest?

    A. 25 Tesla
    B. 35 Tesla
    C. 45 Tesla
    D. 55 Tesla

This question is chock-full of useless information. The test writers
love to introduce extraneous information in their questions because
they know it makes the questions intimidating. Don't get trapped. Cut
your way through the nonsense to find out what is important and then
do the question.

In this question all they're saying is that a high potential difference decreases the time that a particle needs to move. They want to
know which magnetic field would cause the lowest potential difference. Well, we've been dealing with just that issue on the previous
two questions, so it should be pretty clear by now that a decrease in
field strength causes a decrease in potential difference; the answer
must be A.

6. How would one best investigate the effect of
the bar's thickness on the potential difference
between the two ends?

    F. Use bars of the same thickness rotating at
different angular velocities.
    G. Use identical bars made out of different
materials.
    H. Use both very short and very long bars.
    J. Use cylindrical bars of varying radii.

Any time the ACT asks you what the best way to study something is,
the answer is always the same—mess with whatever it is you want to
study. If you want to investigate the effect of temperature on something, run a bunch of trials at different temperatures. If you want to

investigate the effect of thickness, then run a bunch of trials that vary the thickness. The only answer that plays around with the thickness of the bars is J.

Fighting Scientists

Each Science test will have one fighting scientists passage. This passage will always have seven questions and can come at any point in the section. There are two major ways in which it is different from the other passages. First, it usually doesn't have graphs or charts of any kind. Second, all of the written material they give you, including the scientists' arguments, is important and must be read.

Every fighting scientists passage features a number of scientists debating some issue. There are usually two or three viewpoints represented (although we've seen as many as five), and the topic can be anything from the timely to the ridiculous. What you must remember is that the topic is irrelevant. For example, if the topic is life on Mars, and one scientist is saying that Mars is clearly inhabited by green men, it doesn't matter that we know that it's not. What matters is understanding how the argument is constructed, because that's what the questions will hinge on. You need to know how each argument is put together and what each scientist's point is.

The Big Technique: Read Carefully

When you get to the fighting scientists passage, you are in for some reading. It's the only way to do the questions. This alone may be enough to make you decide to put this passage last when you reorder the passages. That's fine, but when you get to it, you'll still have to read it.

There are two parts to a fighting scientists passage: the introduction and the hypotheses. First read the introduction, because it will set the stage for you. Then, read each hypothesis—carefully. Fortunately, they are pretty short—usually about 20 lines long.

As you read a hypothesis, note each of the supporting points, either on the side or by underlining within the hypothesis. When you get to the end of a hypothesis, ask yourself what it was about. If you can't quickly restate the scientist's position to yourself, you weren't paying enough attention when you read it. Go back and read it again. You must understand what is being said in order to do the questions.

The Questions

The questions come in two varieties: those that are concerned with only one hypothesis and those that are concerned with multiple hypotheses. Usually, there are three of the former type and four of the latter. Do the questions that deal with a single hypothesis first. All of the questions are done in the same way as reading questions, which you already learned about in Step 7.

Step 1—Read the Question
When you read the question, put it into your own words before going to the passage to find the answer.

Step 2—Find the Answer in the Passage
Use the line reference or lead word to locate the part of the passage with the answer in it. Read there until you've figured out the answer.

Step 3—Put the Answer into your Own Words
This is the most important step. You must put the answer into your own words before you go back to look at the answer choices. You do this to confirm that you really understand what you're reading and to avoid falling for any of the traps that are waiting in the wrong answer choices.

Step 4—POE
Read the answers and cross off any that don't agree with your answer.

Let's try it all out on the following fighting scientists passage. We'll start off by reading the introduction:

> One of the great controversies in the history of science was over what happens when things burn. Below, two scientists present their views on this matter.

Reading this introduction tells you what the scientists are going to be debating—how burning things works. On to the first hypothesis. As you read it, note the points of the argument, and when you're at the end, paraphrase the point of the argument.

Scientist 1

Any substance capable of burning possesses some predetermined amount of an invisible fluid called *phlogiston*. The more phlogiston a substance has, the longer it can burn. As the burning occurs, the object loses phlogiston. Finally, when there is no phlogiston left, the object stops burning. Although phlogiston explains why different objects burn longer than others, it does not explain why some objects known to possess phlogiston will not burn under certain circumstances. To get an object to begin burning at all, it must be in contact with *fire air*, a component of the air we breathe every day. This explains why objects placed in a vacuum (that is, a region of space devoid of all air) will not burn. Although the objects may have enough phlogiston inside them to sustain the burning process, there is no fire air inside a vacuum, so the object will not burn.

Crash Course for the ACT

The important things you should have noted in this hypothesis are that phlogiston is what causes things to burn; that when it's gone, burning stops; and that fire air is also needed for combustion. Never mind that we know all of this is untrue (although it was the accepted theory prior to the discovery of oxygen). All that matters is that you understood the argument.

Here's the other hypothesis. Repeat the process of reading while noting the points being made:

Scientist 2

The only thing necessary for *combustion* (the chemical process of burning) is the element oxygen. Normally present in the air around us, there is usually an almost unlimited supply of oxygen anywhere near a burning object. When an object burns, it is undergoing a chemical reaction with the oxygen in the air. The products of such a reaction will then be different chemical compounds that have oxygen atoms in them (and perhaps other compounds not involving oxygen). Experimentally, we see that objects that burn are heavier afterward. Thus, something must have been added to them. This something is oxygen. The energy that a combustion reaction produces (in the form of heat) is the energy that was stored in the chemical bonds in the substance beforehand. When these bonds are broken, the energy must go elsewhere, and it is released as heat energy.

This second hypothesis says that oxygen is the component necessary for combustion. Supporting points you should have noted are that oxygen is in air, that things get heavier when they burn, and that the heat of fire is energy coming from the bonds being broken. If any of this eluded you, you need to reread the hypothesis now.

The questions for the fighting scientists passage are handled like those on the Reading test, so let's dive right in with a question that refers to only one of the two hypotheses:

> **1.** How would Scientist 2 explain why objects placed in a vacuum do not burn?

Why don't things burn in a vacuum? When you were reading the hypothesis, you noted that Scientist 2 said that oxygen is necessary for combustion. There's no oxygen in a vacuum. That's the answer in your own words, so let's go to the answer choices:

> **A.** There is no oxygen in a vacuum.
> **B.** There is no fire air in a vacuum.
> **C.** There is no phlogiston in a vacuum.
> **D.** Chemical reactions cannot take place in a vacuum.

Choices B and C are both from Scientist 1. This will happen all the time on fighting scientists. Choice D is wholly irrelevant to what we're doing, and A is pretty much exactly what we came up with before we looked at the answer choices, so it's the one we want. Choice A is correct.

Here's another:

> **2.** Wood burns for a greater length of time than does newspaper. How would Scientist 1 explain this fact?

Okay, Scientist 1 was the phlogiston guy. Go back to your notes for that hypothesis. He said that things burn until all the phlogiston is gone, so he would probably say that wood has more phlogiston in it than paper does. On to the answers.

> **F.** Wood reacts with oxygen more quickly than newspaper does.
> **G.** Wood reacts with oxygen more slowly than newspaper does.
> **H.** Wood has more phlogiston than newspaper does.
> **J.** Wood has less phlogiston than newspaper does.

Again, notice how there are answers from the wrong hypothesis. Both F and G are talking about oxygen, which Scientist 1 never even mentions. Eliminate them immediately. Choices H and J are opposites, and H agrees with what we said, so it is correct.

Questions involving both scientists usually ask about the similarities and differences of the hypotheses. That's why we told you to note the building blocks of the arguments as you read the hypotheses. Sometimes you'll be asked how one scientist would react to another scientist's argument. That tests the same thing—your understanding of the underlying arguments.

Here's a multiscientist question for you:

3. Which of the following is explained by Scientist 2 but not by Scientist 1?
   A. Why some objects burn longer than others
   B. Why fires are hot
   C. Why some objects burn but others do not
   D. Why objects placed in a vacuum do not burn

The only way to tackle questions like these is from the answer choices. POE is the way to go. It's especially important to keep your scientists straight. You want to find something Scientist 1 doesn't address but that Scientist 2 does. Choice D is easy to eliminate because both scientists mentioned vacuums. Choice A is quickly gone, too, because Scientist 1 says clearly that burn time is related to phlogiston content. Choice C is also out, because Scientist 1 says at the beginning that the only things that can burn are those that contain phlogiston. That leaves B. Scientist 2 does, in fact, explain why fires are hot (it's actually one of the things we noted when reading the hypothesis), but Scientist 1 never talks about this. Choice B is correct.

4. What is the most dramatic difference between the theories of Scientist 1 and Scientist 2?

F. Scientist 2 postulates the existence of phlogiston, whereas Scientist 1 does not.

G. Scientist 1 provides an explicit definition of combustion, whereas Scientist 2 does not.

H. Scientist 1 says that burning objects lose something, but Scientist 2 says that something gets added to burning objects.

J. Scientist 2 provides an accurate description of the chemical composition of air, but Scientist 1 does not.

Once again, keeping the scientists straight is essential to getting the question right. Scientist 1 was the phlogiston guy, and Scientist 2 was the oxygen guy. That means F is out immediately. G is backward, too; Scientist 2 starts off by defining combustion, so eliminate it. That leaves H and J.

Choice H seems pretty good. Scientist 1 said phlogiston leaves burning things, and Scientist 2 said oxygen is added to burning things. Let's look at J. Scientist 1 didn't provide an accurate description of much of anything, so that's true, but did Scientist 2 provide an accurate description of the chemical composition of air? No. All he did was say that air contains oxygen. He didn't mention any of the other components of air. Choice J is out. Choice H is the correct answer.

Step 10:
ACT Writing Test

The ACT Writing test is an "optional" test that comes after the Science test. Does that mean *you* decide whether to take the Writing test? Not really; it all depends on the colleges to which you're applying. Before you concern yourself with the contents of this chapter, be sure to check ACT's website to see if your target schools recommend or require the Writing test. If you aren't sure whether you'll need the Writing test, it's probably safest to sign up for it. You can't sign up for just the Writing test, and the last thing you'd want to do is take the entire ACT again if you don't have to!

Overview

The ACT Writing test is a 30-minute section with one essay prompt. You must pay an additional fee to take this portion of the ACT, and test takers who do write the essay are usually put into a separate room from those who don't. When you take the Writing test, you will receive two additional scores on your score report. First, you'll see the Writing test score (which is scored on a 1–36 scale), as well as four subscores (ideas and analysis, development and support, organization, and language use). These subscores will be scored and reported on a 2–12 scale. Second, you'll get a combined English/Writing/Reading score called the English Language Arts Score. The most important thing for you to know, however, is that Writing test score and subscores, and the English Language Arts Score do not factor into your composite. English, Math, Reading, and Science are still the only scores reflected in the composite number.

Essay Scoring

According to ACT, each essay is evaluated on how well it exhibits your ability to do the following:

- analyze different points of view on a complex issue

- develop your position using logical reasoning, prior knowledge, and experience

- develop a position by using logical reasoning and by supporting your ideas

- organize ideas in a logical way
- use language clearly and effectively according to the rules of standard written English

The four subscores will be graded along the following guidelines:

Ideas and Analysis: This score is determined by how well you understand and analyze the different perspectives and by the quality of your own ideas.

Development and Support: This score reflects how well you develop and explore your ideas using reasoning and examples.

Organization: This score is determined by how well you organize your essay.

Language Use and Conventions: This score will reflect the grammar and style of your writing.

The Big Technique: Be a Top Half Writer

Because your essay is graded holistically, it is in your best interest to make a strong, immediate impression upon the reader. If your essay receives a "top half" score you will end up with a solid Writing test score. The first step to a top half score is ensuring that your essay adheres to these three simple guidelines:

> **Length:** Be sure to write as much as you can in the time allotted. While a long essay certainly won't guarantee a high score, a short essay is unlikely to give the reader the impression that you've given the prompt adequate consideration.

> **Legibility:** Under a timed circumstance, writers often tend to scribble more than usual. Be sure to present a neatly written response! If the reader can't decipher your sentences, he or she is unlikely to view your essay in the most favorable light.

Appearance: From a holistic standpoint, an essay that looks well-structured is a plus. Make sure you avoid inserting text or crossing out words if you can. Indent your paragraphs and keep your introduction, body paragraphs, and conclusion separate from each other.

Let's analyze a top half score to analyze what exactly you should do to earn a top half score.

> Many societal changes come about as a result of conflict. A single act of persecution or violence towards an individual can spark widespread protests demanding change in an oppressive government. On a smaller scale, students at a school or employees in a workplace may feel dissatisfied with the way things are run and lobby for a change in policies. Many times such conflicts result in positive changes, but is disagreement necessary to evoke change? Given the number of social issues that cause strong emotional reactions from multiple sides, it is worth examining the implications of such conflict.

Read and carefully consider these perspectives. Each suggests a particular way of thinking about the role of conflict in social change.

Perspective One	Perspective Two	Perspective Three
If people are not in some way dissatisfied with their situations in life, change will never happen. Motivation to act for change can come only from righteous indignation.	Heated conflicts rarely result in lasting change. On the contrary, those in charge are more likely to respond to civil and constructive conversation than to attacks.	Much positive change comes about without conflict at all. When people are content, they are better able to work together to further improve society.

Essay Task

Write a unified, coherent essay in which you evaluate multiple perspectives on the role of conflict. In your essay, be sure to

- analyze and evaluate the perspectives given
- state and develop your own perspective on the issue
- explain the relationship between your perspective and those given

Your perspective may be in full agreement with any of the others, in partial agreement, or wholly different. Whatever the case, support your ideas with logical reasoning and detailed, persuasive examples.

For starters, let's look at the instructions in the prompt. These directions never change, so you'll always need to do the following things:

- Analyze and evaluate the perspectives given
- State and develop your own perspective on the issue
- Explain the relationship between your perspective and those given

Although there are certainly more facets to a well-written essay than the three points above, we can use these as a springboard for constructing a top half essay. Below, you can see a sample essay response that received a score of 18. Let's see how this student addresses the issue of whether or not conflict should be used as an agent of change.

Part I: The Intro

I believe that conflict is necessary for change. When a person is satisfied with their position in life, they have no reason to make changes. The most important social changes happen when there is direct conflict with authority; civil conversation often isn't enough. Direct conflict can result in widespread support for an overhaul of the way things are, such as in the Civil Rights movement and the American Revolution.

Although it may not be the most complete introduction you've ever read, this paragraph accomplishes a few important goals. First, the writer clearly takes a position on the issue and is in agreement with the first perspective given in the prompt. Second, the other two perspectives in the prompt are briefly addressed. Third, the writer tells the reader why direct conflict is necessary. The reasons presented clearly foreshadow what will be discussed in the body paragraphs.

Part II: The Body

The idea that conflict is necessary for change can be seen through the example of the Civil Rights movement. Because African Americans were unhappy with the idea of "separate but equal," they are able to successfully lobby for a change. When Rosa Parks refused to give up her seat on a bus, her simple act of disobedience sparked a bus boycott that eventually became a landmark case in the struggle for civil rights. If African Americans had never protested against the unfair segregation laws, the Civil Rights Act would never have passed.

Some people believe that violent conflict is counterproductive. This situation was clearly demonstrated in the events leading up the American Revolution. When Great Britain imposed a variety of taxes on the American colonies, many colonists wanted to sever all ties with Britain and a series of riots and massacres broke out. However, many colonists did not want to be in direct conflict with Great Britain; instead, they wanted to mend their relationship with King George through compromise and discussion. One view on the role of conflict in change would say that such violence doesn't help any cause and the colonists were worsening their own situation by doing it. But the violence of the riots and the American Revolution eventually led to the creation of the United States, it is now the most powerful nation in the world. The United States would have never become the country it is today if not for that initial conflict.

While it is true that some change, such as increased enforcement of Civil Rights law, happens over time without major conflict, change happens more quickly and more effectively when there is conflict to draw people's attention to the matter at hand. If African Americans in the 50s had not been dissatisfied with segregation, they would not have worked to change it. Similarly, if the American colonists hadn't thought there was a problem with "taxation without representation," they wouldn't have started the American Revolution.

The first paragraph supports the writer's position that conflict is necessary for change by using a specific example. What do you notice about the details given to support this example? The inclusion of a specific act of civil disobedience enhances the general claim by providing some concrete information.

In the second body paragraph, the writer addresses the second perspective included in the prompt, which argues that heated conflict rarely causes real change. The author is able to refute this perspective using another concrete example, the American Revolution. Similarly, the third body paragraph discusses the third perspective, which argues that change can occur without conflict at all. The writer argues against this perspective by drawing from and expanding upon both of the previous examples.

Overall, the body paragraphs are well-structured and use clear transitions to move from one point to the next. You'll notice that this student's grammar is not perfect, but a few errors are considered normal, given the time allotted for drafting the essay. You do want to try to keep your grammar and spelling as clean as possible, but it's not a huge factor in your score. Most of all, it's important for the essay to maintain focus by sticking to the reasons put forth in the introduction, and this essay does a good job of staying on track. Now let's look at the conclusion:

Part III: The Conclusion

> In conclusion, as can be seen through the examples of some landmark moments in the Civil Rights movement, change comes about more effectively as the result of conflict.

Although the conclusion is quite short, it meets the standard the writer needs to earn a top half score. The writer restates his or her position on the issue and mentions the reasons cited in the body paragraphs. If you find yourself with this short of a conclusion, it's likely that you ran out of time. Be sure to outline your essay and stick to the plan before you start writing.

We've done some pretty focused analysis of this essay in order to get an idea of what should be accomplished in each portion of your response. You may not have been awed by the level of detail or rhetorical flourish, but our goal here isn't to win the Pulitzer Prize. Below, we've reproduced the entire essay; pretend you're a holistic grader and read through the essay. Give yourself about two minutes, and think about your overall impression of the writer's response.

> I believe that conflict is necessary for change. When a person is satisfied with their position in life, they have no reason to make changes. The most important social changes happen when there is direct conflict with authority; civil conversation often isn't enough. Direct conflict can result in widespread support for an overhaul of the way things are, such as in the Civil Rights movement and the American Revolution.
>
> The idea that conflict is necessary for change can be seen through the example of the Civil Rights movement. Because African Americans were unhappy with the idea

of "separate but equal," they were able to successfully lobby for a change. When Rosa Parks refused to give up her seat on a bus, her simple act of disobedience sparked a bus boycott that eventually became a landmark case in the struggle for civil rights. If African Americans had never protested against the unfair segregation laws, the Civil Rights Act would never have passed.

Some people believe that violent conflict is counterproductive. This situation was clearly demonstrated in the events leading up the American Revolution. When Great Britain imposed a variety of taxes on the American colonies, many colonists wanted to sever all ties with Britain and a series of riots and massacres broke out. However, many colonists did not want to be in direct conflict with Great Britain; instead, they wanted to mend their relationship with King George through compromise and discussion. One view on the role of conflict in change would say that such violence doesn't help any cause and the colonists were worsening their own situation by doing it. But the violence of the riots and the American Revolution eventually led to the creation of the United States, the most powerful nation in the world. The United States would have never become the country it is today if not for that initial conflict.

While it is true that some change, such as increased enforcement of Civil Rights law, happens over time without major conflict, change happens more quickly and more effectively when there is conflict to draw people's attention to the matter at hand. If African Americans in the 50s had not been dissatisfied with segregation, they would not have worked to change it. Similarly, if the American colonists hadn't thought there was a problem with "taxation without representation," they wouldn't have started the American Revolution.

In conclusion, as can be seen through the examples of some landmark moments in the Civil Rights movement, change comes about more effectively as the result of conflict.

Do you think this essay "adequately" responds to the prompt? It is lengthy and well structured; it has a clear introduction and conclusion; the supporting examples are present and have some concrete details; the essay acknowledges the other perspectives and explains how they relate to the writer's position. It uses some transitions; its errors are minimal and do not significantly distract the reader. We could go on, but you get the idea. Top half essays are considered top half because of what they have, while bottom half essays are considered bottom half because of what they lack. As long as you have the basics, your essay should be in the top half. After that, it is all a matter of degree. Take a look at the essay below, which received a score very close to the perfect 36—while all the same components are present, this essay paints a more holistically pleasing picture.

> History is replete with examples of the downtrodden rising up against their oppressors to demand change. Rebellions can be bloody, as Nat Turner's slave rebellion was, or peaceful, like India's struggle for independence from Great Britain under Gandhi. While the levels of violence associated with rebellions vary widely, even peaceful revolutions do not take place unless there is some level of conflict or disagreement between different social strata. When people are satisfied with the status quo, they will not work for change.
>
> It may seem on the surface like the two examples given above are wildly different from each other. Nat Turner's slave rebellion lasted only a few days, and while many white slave owners were killed, the rebels failed to improve their situation. Turner himself was gruesomely dismembered after his execution. But while the immediate results of his uprising were to reinforce the power of whites over their slaves, it is harder to quantify what kind of long-term effect it may have had. News of Turner's rebellion and others like it helped to spread the message to blacks and whites that slaves wanted change. It is true that slavery would likely have been abolished whether or not this one event happened, but if there had been no underlying discontent with the institution of slavery, it might still exist today.

Gandhi's struggle, in contrast to Turner's, lasted throughout his life, was characterized by peaceful protest, and resulted change that can be directly attributed to his actions. But it is a mistake to argue that his brand of non-violent revolution happens without conflict. The people of India were unhappy with British rule and were struggling for their freedom in just the same way that slaves in the United States were fighting for theirs.

Even in a situation where it seems that change is taking place because all parties concerned are working together for a better tomorrow, there must be some underlying level of dissatisfaction driving the change. At my school, students in the National Honor Society recently started an after-school peer-tutoring program where struggling students can come for extra help. There was no protest or violence of any kind involved in starting this program. But if there were no need for it, which is to say that if all students were getting all the help they needed from the system that was already in place, the program wouldn't have been established.

Change appears with many different faces, from the seemingly innocuous to the unspeakably bloody. Though it may seem hard to compare the opposite ends of the spectrum, what all change has in common is some level of discontent. Without that sense that things could be different, change would never happen.

In all honesty, some people will have more trouble understanding this essay than they will have understanding the previous, lower-scoring essay. That's one of the oddities of holistic grading; high scoring essays exhibit a stronger command of language and a rhetorical grasp that allows for complete elaboration of the ideas presented. We're not telling you to be overly florid, but once you're a top half writer, you're going to have to hone your delivery to earn a top-tier score. Here are some quick pointers that you can use to develop your essay response further:

- In your introduction, "grab" the reader by opening with an intriguing statement or rhetorical question. An interesting lead-in will engage a holistic reader early.

- Always start with your strongest example first when writing your body paragraphs. If you've gotten the reader's attention in the introduction, a strong first example will further convince him or her that your essay is an effective one.

- Vary your sentence length. Don't overuse long, complex sentences or short, declarative sentences.

- Utilize different transitions—some variety will make your essay flow both logically and stylistically.

- In your conclusion, retain the focus of the essay without restating everything you've discussed verbatim. Refer to your examples without repeating them exactly, and be sure to mention the other perspectives one last time.

Drills

These drills are divided into sets that correspond with the chapters in the book. Practice the math drills *after* you've read *all* of the math chapters, because some questions corresponding with one chapter might require you to use techniques from another chapter. The same goes for the English and science reasoning drills.

Remember to have your calculator handy for all of the math, and write all over everything, just as you will on the day of the test. Here we go!

Step 1 and Step 2

[1]

I'll never forget the week that I spent

in Tongmen; it was a memorable, exciting,
            1   1
and stimulating seven days. First, though,
                        2
I should explain how I came to be there,

taking a break from work, high in the

mountains of eastern Taiwan.

[2]

I was working in the capital, Taipei

(most capitals are very big cities), as a
                        3
translator for a small translation service.

The work I did was usually pretty boring—

mostly translations of advertisements

for large multinational corporations.

However, something interesting would
    4
need translation, like the patent application

for the combination camping stove/flame

thrower or the letter by the Taiwanese

student who was dumping her British

boyfriend, but most of the time it was ads,

ads, and more ads.

1. **A.** NO CHANGE
   B. spent in Tongmen, it was
   C. spent in Tongmen it was
   D. spent in Tongmen, it was,

2. **F.** NO CHANGE
   G. vacation.
   H. week.
   J. OMIT the underlined portion and end the sentence with a period

3. **A.** NO CHANGE
   B. (the largest city in the tiny island nation of Taiwan)
   C. (which rhymes with "my way")
   D. OMIT the underlined portion

4. **F.** NO CHANGE
   G. Occasionally,
   H. Therefore,
   J. Clearly,

[3]

[1] Three nights a week I would hop on my San Yang 150cc motorcycle and commute from the Taiwan University neighborhood where I worked to the firm's offices in Hsinchu. [2] To liven things up, I took a part-time job tutoring English at a small securities firm. [3] Although the analysts' English skills varied greatly, the classes were still quite lively and, I liked to believe, useful for all involved. [4] There I would spend two hours working, with the analysts on business English and American conversational idioms. [6]

[4]

Naturally, much of the conversational practice revolved around differences between life in America and life in Taiwan. [7] Over the course of these conversations I discovered that one of the analysts was not Chinese, but was a member of one of Taiwan's indigenous tribes, the Taroko. [8]

5. **A.** NO CHANGE
    B. two hours working with the analysts,
    C. two hours working with the analysts
    D. two hours working. With the analysts

6. What is the most logical order for the sentences in paragraph 3?
    F. NO CHANGE
    G. 2, 1, 4, 3
    H. 2, 4, 3, 1
    J. 1, 4, 3, 2

7. The author wishes to add a sentence that illustrates the amusing nature of the conversations he had with the analysts. Which sentence, if added, would best accomplish this goal?

    A. One of their favorite topics was Taiwan's overheated economy.
    B. Through these conversations, I could determine my students' weaknesses and assign drills to help them resolve them.
    C. The conversations frequently revolved around misadventures that had been caused by language problems, such as the time Steve Wang had ordered a cheeseburger only to be served a cheese bagel.
    D. I didn't like the job very much, but I needed the money, so I stuck with it.

8. The author is considering adding a paragraph listing all of the other indigenous tribes of Taiwan and explaining their traditional relationships with one another. Would that be appropriate in the context of this essay?

F. Yes, because the added detail will contribute to the reader's understanding of the diversity of Taiwan's non-Chinese inhabitants.

G. Yes, because authors in general should honor those who are different.

H. No, because the small size of these tribes makes them unimportant.

J. No, because the essay's focus is on an experience the author had with the Taroko, and the extra detail on other tribes would be irrelevant.

[5]

Although most of the residents of
        9
Taiwan are descended from immigrants from China, there are still some of the island's original inhabitants living there, just as there are still Cherokee and other Native Americans living in the U.S. [10] When the Taroko analyst in my class offered me a chance to visit her village, I jumped at the opportunity, eager to learn
    11
more about this unique culture.

[6]

Tongmen is a tiny village with no more than 400 residents located in the mountains of eastern Taiwan, near the port city of Hualien. The land surrounding Tongmen was some of the most beautiful I'd ever seen. Great mountains covered with trees towered and teeming with wild pigs, monkeys, and other animals above brisk Mugua River which came rushing down from its source somewhere near the center of the island. Tucked in the shadow, of these mountains, on a ridge above the river was Tongmen.

9. **A.** NO CHANGE
   B. Because
   C. Seemingly
   D. Surprisingly

10. If the first sentence of paragraph 5 were deleted from the essay, the essay would primarily lose:
    F. an irrelevant detail.
    G. an example that provides contrast to what has been stated previously.
    H. a definition of an unfamiliar term.
    J. an explanation of a particular situation and a transition.

11. **A.** NO CHANGE
    B. jumping
    C. did jump
    D. would have jumped

12. In the interest of clarity of meaning, where should the underlined word be placed in the sentence?
    F. Where it is now
    G. After *mountains*
    H. After *animals*
    J. After *which*

13. **A.** NO CHANGE
    B. shadow of these mountains
    C. shadow, of these mountains
    D. shadow of these mountains,

[7]

The Taroko family I stayed with treated me like one of the family. They took me swimming in the river and <u>we hiked</u> up the mountainsides. The last night I was there, they held a feast in which an entire pig was roasted on a spit. The week was full of experiences I'll never forget.

14. **F.** NO CHANGE
    G. on lovely hikes
    H. for hikes
    J. hiking

15. Upon rereading his essay, the author realizes he has left out a point he wanted to make. Where should he insert the following sentence?

Although the river is a significant source of hydroelectric power, the dam upstream has had no negative effect on the beauty downstream.

    A. At the end of paragraph 1
    B. After the first sentence of paragraph 5
    C. Just before the last sentence of paragraph 6
    D. At the end of paragraph 6

Step 3

1. Which of the following represents the sum of the absolute values of –6.5, 3.2, and $\frac{1}{2}$?
    A. –3.2
    B. –2.8
    C. 2.8
    D. 3.2
    E. 10.2

2. In an effort to determine the makeup of a park's animal inhabitants, a researcher counts the first 100 animals she finds in the park (see graph below). Assuming that this is an accurate sampling of the animal population of the park, and assuming that the park has a total of 3,500 animals in it, how many of the park's animals are squirrels?

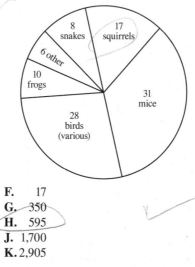

F. 17
G. 350
H. 595
J. 1,700
K. 2,905

3. The average temperature at noon in Olivette over one 10-day period is 74°. If the temperature at noon for each day over the next 10-day period is exactly 6 degrees higher than during the first 10-day period, what is the average temperature for the second 10-day period?

A. 68°
B. 74.6°
C. 76°
D. 80°
E. It cannot be determined from the information provided.

4. What is the sixth term of the geometric sequence
   8, 12, 18, ...?

   F. 30
   G. 36
   H. 40.5
   J. 48
   K. 60.75

5. What is the product of the solutions to the equation
   $|3x - 1| = 10$?

   A. −11
   B. −9
   C. $\dfrac{2}{3}$
   D. 9
   E. 11

6. The greatest common factor of two numbers, x
   and y, is 3. The least common multiple of x and
   y is 18. Which of the following ordered pairs
   correctly gives x and y?

   F. (3,12)
   G. (3,36)
   H. (6,6)
   J. (6,9)
   K. (9,18)

7. Elliot's Apparel pays its employees a weekly
   salary of $150, plus 20% of their sales for that
   week. If Davi earns a total of $400 in one week,
   what were her sales for that week?

   A. $250
   B. $750
   C. $1,250
   D. $1,400
   E. $2,000

8. $|29 - 5| - |5 - 29| = ?$

    F.   0
    G. 24
    H. 35
    J.   48
    K. 58

9. Zoo members receive a 10% discount on all items purchased at the zoo's gift store. If Sabrina is a zoo member, how much will she save if she buys a stuffed panda with a pre-discount price of $75 and a baby-monkey coloring book with a pre-discount price of $12.50? (Ignore tax when calculating your answer.)

    A. $7.50
    B. $8.75
    C. $10.00
    D. $78.75
    E. $87.50

10. The zoo is beginning a new schedule of public feedings for the elephants, gorillas, and bongos. On the first day of the new schedule, all three types of animals will have a public feeding. After that, the elephants will have public feedings every three days, the gorillas will have public feedings every four days, and the bongos will have public feedings every five days. (For example, the elephants' public feedings will be on Day 1, Day 4, Day 7, etc., of the new plan.) How frequently will all three animal groups have public feedings on the same day?

    F. Every 12th day
    G. Every 15th day
    H. Every 20th day
    J. Every 24th day
    K. Every 60th day

11. When the shutter speed of a camera is increased from $\frac{1}{8}$ of a second to $\frac{1}{30}$ of a second, the new shutter speed is what percent faster than the old?

    A. 3.33%
    B. 12.5%
    C. 22%
    D. 73.33%
    E. 350%

12. If 14 is x percent of 350, what is 200% of x?

    F. 0.04
    G. 0.08
    H. 4
    J. 8
    K. 32

13. Cylinder A has a radius of 4 and a volume of 80π. If Cylinder B has the same height as Cylinder A and a radius that is 10% larger than that of Cylinder A, what is the volume of Cylinder B ?

    A. 64.8π
    B. 72π
    C. 88π
    D. 96.8π
    E. 106.48π

Step 4

1. The half-life (the time required for 50% of a substance to undergo radioactive decay) of element A is x days. If the half-life of element B is three times shorter than that of element A and the half-life of element C is 4 days longer than that of element B, then what is the half-life of element C in terms of x?

    A. $\frac{x}{3} - 4$
    B. $\frac{x}{3} + 4$
    C. $\frac{x+4}{3}$
    D. $x - 7$
    E. $3x + 4$

2. The equation $3x^2 - 7x - 6 = 0$ has two solutions. If $x > 0$, what is the value of x?

F. -3

G. $-\dfrac{2}{3}$

H. $\dfrac{2}{3}$

J. 3

K. 6

3. For all $m > 0$, which of the following is equivalent to $\dfrac{2}{m} - \dfrac{3}{4}$?

A. $\dfrac{5}{4}$

B. $-\dfrac{1}{4m}$

C. $\dfrac{8 - 3m}{4m}$

D. $\dfrac{3m - 8}{4m}$

E. $8 - 3m$

4. Which of the following is equivalent to $\dfrac{x+2}{5x^2 + 7x - 6}$?

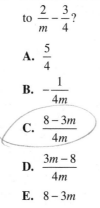

F. $\dfrac{1}{5x - 3}$

G. $\dfrac{1}{5(x-3)}$

H. $\dfrac{1}{5x + 4}$

J. $\dfrac{x+2}{5x-3}$

K. $\dfrac{x+2}{12x-6}$

5. Which of the following points is on the line described by the equation $3x - y = 2$?

   A. $(-1,-5)$
   B. $(0,2)$
   C. $(1,-1)$
   D. $(\frac{3}{2},0)$
   E. $(3,2)$

6. What happens to the value of $d^2 - 1$ as d increases from 0?

   F. It decreases until $d = 1$ and then increases.
   G. It keeps increasing.
   H. It keeps decreasing.
   J. It increases until $d = 1$ and then decreases.
   K. It stays the same.

7. What is the area of a square if the length, p, of each side is tripled?

   A. p^2
   B. $3p^2$
   C. $9p^2$
   D. $9p^4$
   E. $3p^6$

8. If Thad scored x, $x - 2$, $3x + 5$, and $2x + 1$ points in each of his team's last 4 basketball games, what is the average number of points he scored per game over those 4 games?

   F. $7x - 4$
   G. $7x - 1$
   H. $\frac{x}{4}$
   J. $\frac{7}{4}x - 4$
   K. $\frac{7}{4}x + 1$

9. After a 20% discount, a portable stereo is priced at $96.00. What was the original price of the stereo?

   A. $76.00
   B. $76.80
   C. $115.20
   D. $116.00
   E. $120.00

10. If $x^2 + 8x = -16$, what is the value of x?

    F. −8
    G. −6
    H. −4
    J. −2
    K. 0

11. If $\sqrt{2y^2 - 7} = 3 - y$, then what could be the value of y?

    A. −8 and 2 only
    B. 8 and 2 only
    C. −8 only
    D. 2 only
    E. 8 only

12. What is the product of the terms $x + 11$, $x - 1$, and $x - 3$?

    F. $3x - 3$
    G. $x^3 + 3$
    H. $3x^3 + 3$
    J. $-x^3 + 3x^2 + x - 3$
    K. $x^3 - 3x^2 - x + 3$

Step 5

1. If If $x^2 + kx + 12 = 0$, and all solutions for x are integers, all of the following could be the value of k EXCEPT:

   A.   −7
   B.   7
   C.   8
   D.   12
   E.   13

Crash Course for the ACT

2. $\dfrac{j^4 k^2 l}{k^3 l^2} = ?$ $\dfrac{j^4}{kl}$

F. $\dfrac{j^4}{kl}$

G. $j^4 kl$

H. $\dfrac{j^4 k}{l^3}$

J. $\dfrac{j^4 k}{l}$

K. $\dfrac{j^4 k^5}{l}$

3. A car dealership is giving a rebate on all new cars. The rebate is \$40 for each \$1,000 of the car's price. So, for example, a car selling for \$2,000 would have a rebate of \$80. What would the rebate be for a car with a price of \$13,250?

50

A. \$40.00
B. \$132.50
C. \$530.00
D. \$545.00
E. \$620.00

4. If $x = -2$, what is the value of $\dfrac{3 - x^2}{x^2 + 1}$?

F. -5

G. $-\dfrac{7}{5}$

H. $-\dfrac{1}{5}$

J. $\dfrac{1}{5}$

K. 1

5. If $f(x) = 2x^2 - 3x + 1$, what is $f(-1)$?

   A. -4
   B. -1
   C. 0
   D. 2
   E. 6

6. If $-\dfrac{3}{2}x + 2 > -1$, which of the following correctly gives all possible values of x?

   F. $x < -2$
   G. $x > -2$
   H. $x < -\dfrac{2}{3}$
   J. $x > 2$
   K. $x < 2$

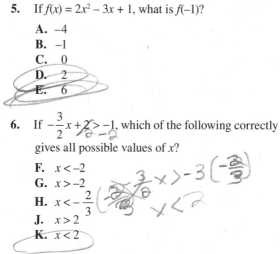

7. On a map of Missouri, the distance between St. Louis and Columbia is 2.5 inches, the distance between Columbia and Hermann is 1.3 inches, and the distance between Hermann and Ironton is .75 inches. If the actual distance between St. Louis and Columbia is 120 miles, then how far apart are Hermann and Ironton, to the nearest tenth of a mile?

   A. 36.0
   B. 60.0
   C. 62.4
   D. 208.0
   E. 230.8

8. What is the sum of the solutions to
   $$6x^2 + 11x - 10 = 0?$$

   F. $-\dfrac{19}{6}$
   G. $-\dfrac{5}{2}$
   H. $-\dfrac{11}{6}$
   J. $-\dfrac{10}{6}$
   K. $\dfrac{2}{3}$

Crash Course for the ACT

9. Which of the following is the correctly factored form of $9a^2 + 18a^3 - 12a^2 - 6a$?

A. $18a^3 - 3a^2 - 6a$
B. $3a(6a^2 - 7a - 2)$
C. $3a(2a + 1)(3a - 2)$
D. $3(6a^3 - a^2 - 2a)$
E. $3a(6a^3 - a^2 - 2a)$

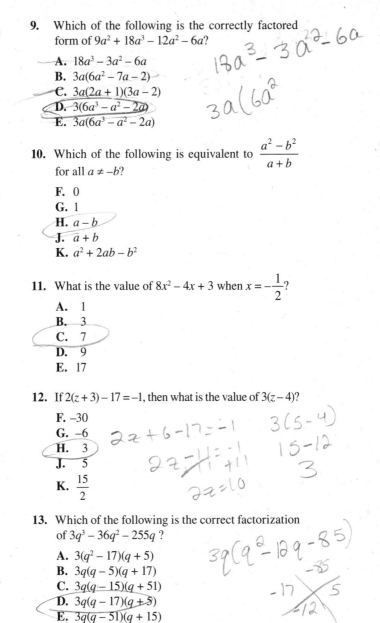

10. Which of the following is equivalent to $\dfrac{a^2 - b^2}{a + b}$ for all $a \neq -b$?

F. 0
G. 1
H. $a - b$
J. $a + b$
K. $a^2 + 2ab - b^2$

11. What is the value of $8x^2 - 4x + 3$ when $x = -\dfrac{1}{2}$?

A. 1
B. 3
C. 7
D. 9
E. 17

12. If $2(z + 3) - 17 = -1$, then what is the value of $3(z - 4)$?

F. −30
G. −6
H. 3
J. 5
K. $\dfrac{15}{2}$

13. Which of the following is the correct factorization of $3q^3 - 36q^2 - 255q$?

A. $3(q^2 - 17)(q + 5)$
B. $3q(q - 5)(q + 17)$
C. $3q(q - 15)(q + 51)$
D. $3q(q - 17)(q + 5)$
E. $3q(q - 51)(q + 15)$

Step 6

1. Bill is painting a wall in his attic with dimensions in feet as shown in the figure below. One gallon of paint will cover 40 square feet of wall. How many square feet of wall does Bill have to paint?

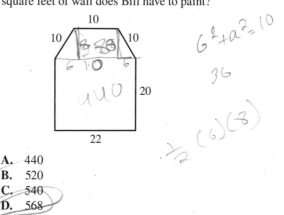

A. 440
B. 520
C. 540
D. 568
E. 616

2. In the triangle below, what is tan$X$?

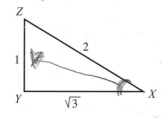

F. $\dfrac{1}{2}$

G. $\dfrac{\sqrt{3}}{2}$

H. $\dfrac{\sqrt{3}}{3}$

J. $\dfrac{2\sqrt{3}}{3}$

K. 2

3. A mechanical watering device sprays water from a long pipe that rotates slowly around a fixed center point. If the pipe is 100 feet long, how far does the outermost end of the pipe travel in one full trip around the field?

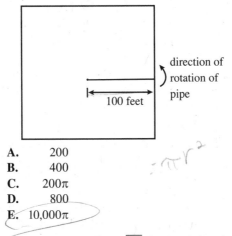

100 feet

direction of rotation of pipe

A. 200
B. 400
C. 200π
D. 800
E. $10,000\pi$

4. What is the length of $\overline{FG}$ in the right triangle depicted below?

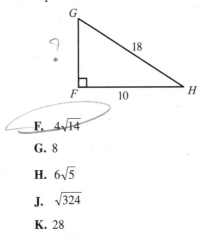

F. $4\sqrt{14}$

G. 8

H. $6\sqrt{5}$

J. $\sqrt{324}$

K. 28

5. What is the slope of a line through points (–2,5) and (3,–1)?

A. $-\dfrac{5}{2}$

B. $-\dfrac{6}{5}$

C. $-\dfrac{5}{6}$

D. $\dfrac{1}{4}$

E. $\dfrac{4}{1}$

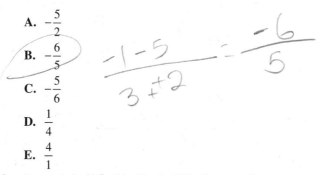

$\dfrac{-1-5}{3+2} = \dfrac{-6}{5}$

6. A round clock face in Ms. Smith's classroom has a diameter of 12 inches. If the lines marking the hours are exactly on the edge of the clock face, what is the distance along the edge from the line indicating 2 o'clock to the line indicating 4 o'clock? Give your answer to the nearest hundredth.

F. 3.14
G. 6.28
H. 9.42
J. 18.85
K. 37.70

7. What is the slope of a line which goes through the point (2,–3) and is perpendicular to the line represented by $5x - 3y = 2$?

A. $-\dfrac{5}{3}$

B. $-\dfrac{3}{5}$

C. $\dfrac{3}{5}$

D. $\dfrac{3}{2}$

E. $\dfrac{5}{3}$

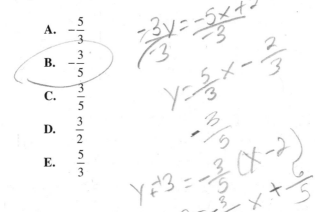

$-3y = \dfrac{-5x+2}{-3}$

$y = \dfrac{5}{3}x - \dfrac{2}{3}$

$-\dfrac{3}{5}$

$y+3 = -\dfrac{3}{5}(x-2)$

$y+3 = -\dfrac{3}{5}x + \dfrac{6}{5}$

$y+3 = -\dfrac{3}{5}x + \dfrac{6}{5}$

Crash Course for the ACT

8. What is the distance in the standard coordinate plane between (–2,5) and (3,3)?

   F. 7
   G. $\sqrt{29}$
   H. 5
   J. 2
   K. $\dfrac{2}{5}$

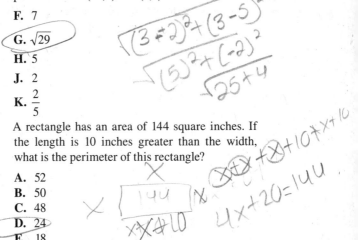

9. A rectangle has an area of 144 square inches. If the length is 10 inches greater than the width, what is the perimeter of this rectangle?

   A. 52
   B. 50
   C. 48
   D. 24
   E. 18

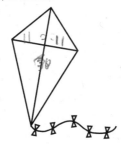

10. A kite (pictured below) is braced with two pieces of balsa wood, one 22 inches long and the other 30 inches long. The two braces cross at a point 10 inches from the top of the kite, forming four right angles. What is the area of the diamond created by the kite, in inches?

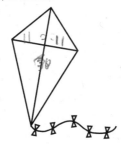

   F. 75.38
   G. 104
   H. 330
   J. 440
   K. 660

11. In triangle ABC, the length of hypotenuse $\overline{AC}$ is 10 and $\sin A = \dfrac{4}{5}$. What is the length of $\overline{AB}$?

   A. 3
   B. 4
   C. 5
   D. 6
   E. 8

12. Which of the following equations represents a line perpendicular to the line given by $6 = 4x - 2y$?

   F. $x + y = 3$
   G. $x - 2y = 10$
   H. $4y - 2x = 20$
   J. $6 + 2y = -x$
   K. $6y = 3x + 12$

Step 7

The first seven questions of the reading drills are based on the World's Fairs passage printed on pages 121–122. That passage is not reprinted here, so go get it because you'll need it to do these questions.

1. The author suggests that the timing of the four World's Fairs was:

   A. ironic.
   B. admirable.
   C. contemptible.
   D. unrealistic.

2. According to the passage, the Golden Gate Exposition and the New York World's Fair were both notable for:

   F. bringing in record numbers of visitors.
   G. having extraordinarily long runs.
   H. losing huge amounts of money.
   J. bridging two eras of history.

3. According to the passage, which of the fairs had the greatest attendance?

   A. Chicago's "Century of Progress"
   B. The New York World's Fair
   C. San Francisco's Golden Gate Exposition
   D. The Texas Centennial Exposition

4. The exhibits shown at the U.S. World's Fairs portrayed Americans as:

   F. unimaginative.
   G. realistic.
   H. ambitious.
   J. timid.

5. The New York World's Fair was inspired by which of the following events?

   I.   The success of Chicago's World's Fair
   II. The inauguration of George Washington
   III. A vision of world peace

   A. I only
   B. II only
   C. I and II only
   D. I and III only

6. All of the following statements concerning Chicago's World Fair are true EXCEPT:

   F. It was the first World's Fair of the decade in the U.S.
   G. It promoted progress made during the twentieth century.
   H. It was a source of pride for Chicago's citizens.
   J. It generated a significant profit.

7. According to the passage, which of the World's Fairs took place in two cities?

   A. The New York World's Fair
   B. The "Century of Progress" celebration
   C. The Texas Centennial Exposition
   D. The Golden Gate Exposition

Drawing is a curious process, so intertwined with seeing that the two can hardly be separated. Ability to draw depends on ability to see the way an artist sees, and this kind of
5   seeing can marvelously enrich your life.

In many ways, teaching drawing is somewhat like teaching someone to ride a bicycle. It is very difficult to explain in words. In teaching someone to ride a
10 bicycle, you might say, "Well, you just get on, push the pedals, balance yourself, and off you'll go."

Of course, that doesn't explain it at all, and you are likely finally to say, "I'll get on
15 and show you how. Watch and see how I do it."

And so it is with drawing. Most art teachers and drawing textbook authors exhort beginners to "change their ways of looking at things" and to "learn how
20 to see." The problem is that the teacher often ends by saying, in effect, "Look at these examples and just keep trying. If you practice a lot, eventually you may get it." While nearly everyone learns to ride
25 a bicycle, many individuals never solve the problems of drawing. To put it more precisely, most people never learn to *see* well enough to draw.

Because only a few individuals seem to
30 possess the ability to see and draw, artists
are often regarded as persons with a rare
God-given talent. To many people, the
process of drawing seems mysterious and
somehow beyond human understanding.

35   Artists themselves often do little to
dispel the mystery. If you ask an artist (that
is, someone who draws well as a result of
either long training or chance discovery of
the artist's way of seeing), "How do you
40 draw something so that it looks real—say a
portrait or a landscape?" the artist is likely to
reply, "Well, I just have a gift for it, I guess,"
or "I really don't know. I just start in and
work things out as I go along," or "Well, I
45 just *look* at the person (or the landscape) and
I draw what I see." The last reply seems like
a logical and straightforward answer. Yet,
on reflection, it clearly doesn't explain the
process at all, and the sense that the skill of
50 drawing is a vaguely magical ability persists.

While this attitude of wonder at artistic
skill causes people to appreciate artists and
their work, it does little to encourage individuals to try to learn to draw; and it doesn't
55 help teachers explain to students the process
of drawing. Often, in fact, people even feel
that they shouldn't take a drawing course
because they don't already know how to
draw. This is like deciding you shouldn't
60 take a French class because you don't
already speak French.

The magical mystery of drawing ability seems to be, in part at least, an ability to make a shift in brain state to a different
65 mode of seeing/perceiving. *When you see in the special way in which experienced artists see, then you can draw.* This is not to say that the drawings of great artists such as Leonardo da Vinci or Rembrandt are
70 not still wondrous because we may know something about the cerebral process that went into their creation. Indeed, scientific research makes master drawings seem even more remarkable because they seem to cause
75 a *viewer* to shift to the artist's mode of perceiving. But the basic skill of drawing is also accessible to everyone who can learn to make the shift to the artist's mode and see in the artist's way.

80   Drawing is not really difficult. *Seeing* is the problem, or, to be more specific, shifting to a *particular way of seeing*. By making a mental shift a twofold advantage is gained: first, accessing by *conscious volition* to the
85 right side of the brain in order to experience a slightly altered mode of awareness; second, to see things in a different way.

    Many artists have spoken of seeing things differently when drawing and have
90 often mentioned that drawing puts them into a somewhat altered state of awareness. In that different subjective state, artists speak of feeling transported, "at one with the work," able to grasp relationships that

95 they ordinarily cannot grasp. Awareness of
the passage of time fades away, and words
recede from consciousness. Artists say that
they feel alert and aware yet are relaxed and
free of anxiety, experiencing a pleasurable,
100 almost mystical activation of the mind.

The state of feeling transported, which
most artists experience, is a state probably
not altogether unfamiliar to you. You may
have observed in yourself slight shifts in
105 your state of consciousness while engaged
in much more ordinary activities than art
work. For example, most people are aware
that they occasionally slip from ordinary
waking consciousness into the slightly
110 altered state of daydreaming. As another
example, people often say that reading takes
them "out of themselves."

The key to learning to draw, therefore, is
to *set up* conditions that cause you to make a
115 mental shift to a different mode of information processing—the slightly altered state
of consciousness—that enables you to see
well. In this *drawing mode* you will be able
to draw your perceptions even though you
120 may never have studied drawing. Once the
drawing mode is familiar to you, you will be
able to consciously control the mental shift.

1. According to the author, Rembrandt and da Vinci:

   A. had larger brains than most people.
   B. drew no better than can most people when properly taught.
   C. had better eyesight than most artists.
   D. viewed their surroundings in a unique way.

2. The author draws an analogy between learning to draw and learning to ride a bicycle on the basis that:

   F. both are physically exhausting.
   G. both are difficult for a teacher to explain verbally to a student.
   H. neither can be learned unless one has an innate talent in that area.
   J. both are well worth the effort.

3. In line 101, the word "transported" is used to mean:

   A. moved from one place to another.
   B. engaged in artistic activity.
   C. in an altered state of consciousness.
   D. dreaming.

4. The main idea of the seventh paragraph (lines 51–61) is that:

   F. anyone who can learn French can learn to draw.
   G. a person cannot appreciate art unless he or she knows how to draw.
   H. people's admiration for art motivates them to learn how to draw.
   J. people who do not know how to draw should not feel intimidated about taking a drawing class.

5. According to the author, the key to learning to draw is to:

   A. find a great artist to be one's mentor.
   B. learn to change one's state of awareness.
   C. study the work of great artists.
   D. focus only on certain objects in one's surroundings.

6. The author says that "*Seeing* is the problem" (lines 80–82) because:

    F. an artist must learn to use a specific area of the brain to view his or her surroundings.

    G. drawing places an enormous strain on the eyes.

    H. the eyes of an artist must be connected to his or her brain in a very specific way.

    J. a person who is color blind can never be an artist.

7. According to the passage, drawing is perceived as all of the following EXCEPT:

    A. a natural talent.

    B. an extremely difficult skill to learn.

    C. less difficult than seeing as an artist does.

    D. intellectually challenging.

8. The state of consciousness that an artist experiences while in the process of creation is most similar to that which an average person experiences while:

    F. solving a complicated math problem.

    G. daydreaming.

    H. chatting with a friend.

    J. being interviewed by a potential employer.

9. According to the passage, the process of drawing is fundamentally linked to that of:

    A. seeing.

    B. imagining.

    C. remembering.

    D. returning to a child-like state.

10. According to the passage, while in the process of drawing, many artists can:

    F. understand concepts that they cannot understand at other times.

    G. work with tremendous speed.

    H. remember scenes and people from their childhood.

    J. carry on complicated conversations with those around them.

Step 8

In an attempt to examine any relationships between *anthropogenic* (man-made) CO_2 and global temperature increase, a researcher has constructed the following diagram. Included in the data are the occurrences of volcanic eruptions which reached the stratosphere, characterized by high dust veil index: Gunung Agung in 1963, Fuego in 1974, El Chichon in 1982, Nevado del Ruiz in 1985, and Pinatubo in 1991.

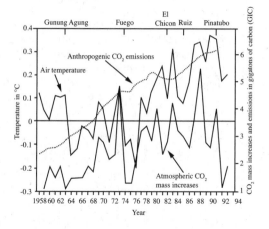

1. According to the information provided about CO_2, anthropogenic emissions and atmospheric mass increases were equal in:

    A. 1968
    B. 1973
    C. 1977
    D. 1986

2. Global air temperatures decreased immediately after some volcanic eruptions. This is due to:

   F. decreased anthropogenic emissions of CO_2.
   G. increased anthropogenic emissions of CO_2.
   H. increased mass of atmospheric CO_2.
   J. a dust veil blocking the sun's radiation.

3. According to the graph, over time, the number of gigatons of carbon entering the atmosphere from man-made sources has:

   A. increased.
   B. decreased.
   C. decreased then increased.
   D. remained constant.

4. From the information provided, changes in global air temperature are dependent on:

   I. anthropogenic emissions
   II. volcanic eruptions
   III. atmospheric mass increases

   F. I only
   G. I and II only
   H. II and III only
   J. I and III only

5. Atmospheric CO_2 mass increases are typically less than anthropogenic emissions. This indicates:

   A. volcanic eruptions may absorb CO_2.
   B. most CO_2 is produced non-anthropogenically.
   C. not all CO_2 emissions are absorbed into the atmosphere.
   D. anthropogenic emissions are warmer than atmospheric mass increases.

Step 9

Passage I

Heat transfer can occur via one of three processes: conduction, convection, or radiation. The easiest of these to describe quantitatively is conduction, which is heat transfer through molecular or atomic collisions. Something one can measure experimentally is the rate at which heat gets transferred through a rod where the two ends are at different temperatures. Of course, in this case, heat will flow from the warmer end to the colder end. If the two ends were at the same temperature, the bar would be at *equilibrium* and heat would not flow through it at all. In the following experiments, scientists measured the heat transfer rates of different rods of known length, cross-sectional area, and *thermal conductivity* (a physical constant that depends only on the material used).

Experiment 1

In this experiment, the scientists kept one end of an iron bar at a temperature of $0°$ C, changed the temperature of the other end, and measured the heat transfer rate. The bar used was 1 m long with a cross-sectional area of 0.5 m^2.

Temperature of other end (°C)	Heat Transfer Rate (Watts)
1.0	39.7
2.0	79.4
3.0	119.1
4.0	158.8
5.0	198.5

Experiment 2

Now, the scientists maintained one end of the bar at 0° C and the other at 2° C, but changed the length of the bar. The cross-sectional area was still 0.5 m².

Length of bar (m)	Heat Transfer Rate (Watts)
0.5	158.8
1.0	79.4
1.5	52.9
2.0	39.7
2.5	31.8
4.0	19.9

Experiment 3

Finally, the scientists took a bar with length 1 m, maintained the temperature at one end at 0° C and the other end at 2° C, and obtained the following readings:

Cross-Sectional Area (m²)	Heat Transfer Rate (Watts)
0.5	39.7
1.0	79.4
2.0	158.8
3.0	238.2
4.0	317.6

1. Based on the information in the passage, one can conclude that when the length of a bar doubles, the heat transfer rate:

   A. halves.
   B. remains the same.
   C. doubles.
   D. quadruples.

2. The scientists hypothesize that thermal conductivity affects heat transfer rate. The best way to test this hypothesis would be to:

   F. repeat experiment 2, but change both the length and cross-sectional area of the bar.
   G. repeat experiment 1, but use even greater temperatures at one of the ends.
   H. do the experiments again using bars made out of different materials.
   J. do the experiments again using cylindrical bars instead of long flat ones.

3. According to the experiments, for a bar 3.0 m long with a cross-sectional area of 0.5 m² and a temperature of 0° C at one end and 2° C at the other, the heat transfer rate would most nearly be:

   A. 238.2 watts
   B. 119.1 watts
   C. 79.4 watts
   D. 26.5 watts

4. Upon further experimentation, scientists discover that it is only the difference in temperatures between the two ends that affects the heat transfer rate. Which of the following pairs of temperatures would produce the same heat transfer rate as 0° C and 2° C in a given bar?

   F. 2° C and 3° C
   G. 5° C and 8° C
   H. 11° C and 13° C
   J. 20° C and 40° C

5. Which of the following graphs best illustrates the relationship between heat transfer rate and length for a bar with given cross-sectional area and temperatures at the two ends?

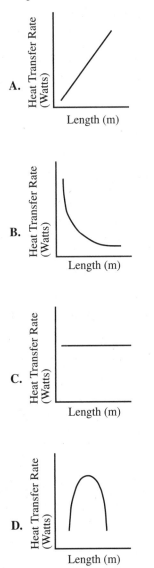

A.

Heat Transfer Rate (Watts)

Length (m)

B.

Heat Transfer Rate (Watts)

Length (m)

C.

Heat Transfer Rate (Watts)

Length (m)

D.

Heat Transfer Rate (Watts)

Length (m)

6. A bar of length 1 m and cross-sectional area 0.5 m^2 has both of its ends maintained at 4° C. What is the heat transfer rate between the two ends?

    F. 39.7 watts
    G. 79.4 watts
    H. 158.8 watts
    J. Heat will not flow between the two ends.

Passage II

For centuries, people have been interested in the nature of light. Seemingly one of the most fundamental things in the universe, its exact nature has been a matter of debate in the scientific community for centuries. Below, three different scientists explain their views on the behavior of light.

The Corpuscular Theory

A beam of light is composed of many small particles (called *corpuscles*) that travel in straight lines through space. When this stream of corpuscles enters the eye, it stimulates the sense of sight. This is how people see light sources. Corpuscles behave in the same way a small ball of matter would. For example, when one shines light on a mirror, the light gets reflected off the mirror with an angle exactly equal to the one with which the light hit the mirror. The same behavior can be seen in billiard balls—when one hits a ball off the side of a pool table, the reflected angle is the same as the incident angle. This provides experimental proof of the corpuscular theory.

The Wave Theory

Light behaves in much the same way as any other waves (for example, water waves and sound waves) do. Like any wave, light requires a *medium* in which to propagate. Waves on the ocean propagate through the medium of water and sound waves propagate through the medium of air. Light propagates through space through the medium of *luminescent ether*, an invisible substance that is undetectable by any known means. There are many known experimental phenomena which only the wave nature of light can explain. For example, it has been shown that light rays can bend around the edges of objects slightly; this is called *diffraction*. Diffraction has been observed for both water waves and sound waves; thus, light must be a wave as well.

The Electromagnetic Theory

Light is merely one type of an *electromagnetic wave*, consisting of changing electric and magnetic fields. Thus, light can travel through a *vacuum*, a region of empty space. The speed of light in a vacuum is almost exactly 3×10^8 meters per second, but the speed of light in different media such as water or glass is always less than this number. Visible light (that is, light humans can see) is merely one type of electromagnetic wave. The color of light depends on its wavelength; the wavelength of visible light ranges from 400 nm (violet) to 700 nm (red), with all other colors in between. Visible light exhibits all familiar properties of wave behavior, such as diffraction, reflection, and refraction.

1. Upon which of the following points do the wave and electromagnetic theories agree?

   A. Light rays consist of a great number of small particles.
   B. There are many instances in which light behaves like a wave.
   C. The color of light depends on its wavelength.
   D. The speed of light is 3×10^8 meters per second.

2. Which of the following predictions of the wave theory would be the most difficult to test experimentally?

   F. Light can bend around the edges of objects.
   G. Water waves and sound waves travel at exactly the same speed.
   H. The existence of luminescent ether.
   J. There exist many other types of electromagnetic waves other than visible light.

3. Which of the following does the corpuscular theory have that the other two theories lack?

   A. An explanation of why there are different colors
   B. An example of something light does that supports its theory
   C. An explanation of why light needs a medium to propagate
   D. An explanation of how sight works.

4. Which of the following assumptions does the author of the electromagnetic theory make?

   F. The speed of light depends on its color.
   G. Electric and magnetic fields can exist in a vacuum.
   H. No one has been able to detect luminescent ether.
   J. Animals can see certain kinds of light that humans cannot.

5. Which of the effects predicted by the wave theory would the corpuscular theory not be able to explain?

   A. The bending of light rays during diffraction
   B. The reflection of light off a mirror
   C. The existence of different colors of light
   D. The speed of light being exactly 3×10^8 meters per second

6. X-rays are a form of electromagnetic wave that behave the same way as light rays. According to the electromagnetic theory, which of the following would be true about X-rays?

   F. X-rays propagate through luminescent ether.
   G. It is impossible for X-rays to bend around the edges of objects.
   H. A human being should not be exposed to X-rays for more than three hours at a time.
   J. X-rays can exhibit diffraction.

7. A scientist does experiments measuring the frequency of visible light and finds that as the frequency increases, the wavelength decreases. What color light would have the lowest frequency?

   A. Violet
   B. Green
   C. Yellow
   D. Red

Step 10

Zoos, facilities that house and display wild animals, have been around since the 19th century. They are still a major presence in cities today: there are currently around 1,000 public zoos around the world. Zoos allow us to view and learn about exotic species we would never have a chance to see in our day-to-day lives. Additionally, zoos protect and breed endangered species that might otherwise die out. However, animal rights activists have long questioned the morality of keeping animals trapped in enclosed spaces. Given the controversy surrounding zoos, it's worth discussing their morality and overall impact.

Read and carefully consider these perspectives. Each suggests a particular way of thinking about the impact and morality of zoos.

Perspective One	Perspective Two	Perspective Three
Bringing animals and humans together is a necessary public service. People are more likely to protect animals if they are able to learn about them and interact with them closely.	Keeping animals confined should be done only when absolutely necessary. We should house and breed the most endangered species, but the ultimate goal should be to return the animals to their natural habitats.	No animals should be imprisoned, even for the good of the species. Animals have individual rights, just like people, and it is immoral to hold them against their will.

Essay Task

Write a unified, coherent essay in which you evaluate multiple perspectives on the morality of zoos. In your essay, be sure to:

- analyze and evaluate the perspectives given
- state and develop your own perspective on the issue
- explain the relationship between your perspective and those given

Your perspective may be in full agreement with any of the others, in partial agreement, or wholly different. Whatever the case, support your ideas with logical reasoning and detailed, persuasive examples.

PART IV

Answers and Explanations

Step 1 and Step 2

1. **A**   The answers tell you this is a punctuation question. Use the Stop/Go tests here. Is the first part a complete idea? Yes. Is the second part a complete idea? Yes. So we need to stop. The only stop punctuation is the semicolon in A.

2. **G**   This is tricky. OMIT is sometimes right, but not this time. The sentence would end strangely if we omitted the underlined part. "Seven days" sounds fine, but so do the other choices. Both F and H are redundant, though: The beginning of the sentence already stated that it was a week, so you don't repeat that later. Choice G is the only choice that's not redundant.

3. **D**   OMIT. If we dump it, does the sentence still work? Yes. Well, do any of the options add something necessary to the essay? No. That capitals are big, Taiwan is tiny, and Taipei rhymes with "my way" are all irrelevant to the story the essay is telling. They may be interesting facts, but they don't fit the narrative.

4. **G**   This is a transition question. The two parts are different, so a contrasting word is needed, but "however" doesn't work here. "Occasionally" is the only other contrasting word.

5. **C**   Another punctuation question. Use the breath test. Would you pause after "working" when saying this sentence? No, so A and D are gone. What about after "analysts"? No again.

6. **G**   Look for two sentences that must follow each other or one sentence that must be first or last. We know sentence 1 has to be after sentence 2 because sentence 1 refers to the firm without explaining what firm he's talking about. It's in sentence 2 that the firm is defined, so F and J are out. Sentence 1 also can't be at the end, so H is out, too.

7. C The question tells you clearly what type of details to add—funny details. You don't even need to look at the passage for this type of question; just eliminate all the non-funny answers. Choice A is about economics and so is not funny. Choice B is about homework, which is also not funny. Choice C sounds sort of funny, and D is not funny at all.

8. J This can be the worst type of question because you have to take time to read the answers pretty carefully. First, answer the yes/no question. Should the author talk about all the tribes of Taiwan? Of course not. This essay is far too narrow in scope for that sort of thing. So, F and G are out. Now you have to read the remaining answers to see which makes the most sense. Choice H is pretty offensive, so it would never be correct. Choice J is a good explanation of why the author shouldn't add those details.

9. A Another transition question. The sentence has a contrast in it, so "Although" will probably work. Choices B and C are definitely out. Does D work better than A? No, it doesn't make sense. It's not surprising at all that most people in Taiwan are Chinese.

10. J Another tough question. If you're pressed for time on the exam, skip it. We have plenty of time, though, so we'll do it. You need to decide how the first sentence in paragraph 5 is acting in the essay. What does it do? Well, it explains how Taiwan has native people like the United States does, and it gets us from paragraph 4 to paragraph 5. Choice F can't be right—the essay is talking about the Taroko, so they're not irrelevant. Choice G is wrong because it's not a contrast of any sort. Choice H seems okay until you think about it—what's the term being explained? What's explained is the situation, not a word. Choice J hits it right on the head.

11. A A verb question. See if the verb is correct in number (yep) and tense (yep).

12. H The only way to do this is to try it in each place. It makes sense only right before "above" and after "animals."

13. B Commas again. Use the breath test. You wouldn't pause after "shadow," so A and C are gone. Pausing after "mountains" is weird, too, so D is out.

14. J Another verb question. The verb we have is correct in number, but what about the tense? The other verb in the sentence is "swimming." Does "hiked" agree with "swimming"? No.

15. C Where did the author talk about a river? Paragraph 6. Eliminate A and B. Find where in the paragraph it would fit.

Step 3

1. E Absolute value means the positive value of something, so change –6.5 to 6.5 and add them up. Don't add them before you change the sign.

2. H Because the graph gives you the distribution of 100 animals, it's just like a percent for each animal. There are 17 squirrels in the first 100 animals, so 17 percent of the animals are squirrels. Because there are really 3,500 animals, not 100, you can ballpark and cross out F because it's too small and J and K because they are both too large—almost half or more. So, you want to find 17 percent of 3,500 to get the total number of squirrels: $(0.17)(3,500) = 595$.

3. D This seems harder than it really is. Either plug in a temperature for each of the ten days so that the average is 74 (we suggest using 74 for every day—it's much easier this way), or realize that because the temperature on every day is 6 degrees higher, the average will also be 6 degrees higher.

4. K In a geometric sequence, you multiply each term by a specific number to find the next, so you need to figure out what that multiplier is here. What times 8 equals 12? That translates to $8x = 12$, so you can solve for $x = \frac{3}{2}$. That's the multiplier. Now, multiply 18 by $\frac{3}{2}$ to get the fourth term. It's 27. Multiply by $\frac{3}{2}$ again to get the fifth term: 40.5. Multiply one more time to get the sixth term: 60.75.

5. A To get the two solutions you have to solve the positive and negative absolute values. Let's do the positive first. $3x - 1 = 10$, so $x = \frac{11}{3}$. The negative one is $3x - 1 = -10$, so $x = -3$. Multiply those together and you get -11.

6. J First, get rid of pairs that have a greatest common factor other than 3. For H, that's 6, so cross it out. For K, it's 9, so cross that out, too. Now deal with the least common multiple. The least common multiple for F is 12 and for G is 36, so the answer is J.

7. C Davi's sales must be much more than what she earned, because she gets only a small percentage of them as her pay, so ballpark and cross out A and B. How much of Davi's pay is from her sales? $400 - 150 = 250$. So 250 is 20 percent of her sales for the week. That translates to $250 = \frac{20}{100}s$. Solve that for $s = 1,250$.

8. F Do what's inside the absolute value operators first, and then make it positive. Each works out to 24. Subtract those and you get 0.

9. B The two items together cost $87.50 before the discount. The question is asking how much her discount is, so eliminate D and E as too large. Use the 10 Percent Rule and you get B by moving the decimal one place to the left.

10. K What's up with all these zoo questions? And what's a bongo, anyway? You can either write out a chart for each animal and see what matches for all three (for elephants you'd write 1, 4, 7, 10, 13, 16, 19, 22, 25, . . . for gorillas you'd write 1, 5, 9, 13, 17, 21, . . . and for bongos you'd write 1, 6, 11, 16, 21, . . .) or multiply the three numbers together to get 60. Matching up multiples is the same thing as finding a lowest common multiple.

11. D Convert the fractions to decimals, subtract them, and put that amount over the original. If you got E, you went in the wrong direction (faster to slower).

12. J Try to ballpark first. 14 is a pretty small part of 350, so x must be a small number. Even when you take 200% of x, or multiply x by 2, it will still be pretty small. To actually solve it, translate the problem to math: $\frac{14}{100} \times 350 = x$. Then use your calculator to solve for x, which should equal 4. Now find 200% of 4: $\frac{200}{100} \times 4 = 2 \times 4 = 8$.

13. D Cylinder B has the same height as Cylinder A and a bigger radius, so the volume of Cylinder B must be greater than that of Cylinder A. Ballpark and get rid of A and B, which are smaller than 80π. The radius of B is only 10% larger than that of A, so E is too big. By the 10 Percent Rule, D is 10% larger than the volume of Cylinder A, but it was the radius, not the volume that increased by 10%. So D is a good bet for the right answer. To solve this, find the height of Cylinder A. Volume = $\pi r^2 h = \pi(4)^2 h = 80\pi$. Solve for h to get $h = 5$. Use the 10 Percent Rule to find that the radius of Cylinder B is 4.4; then plug the numbers into the volume formula: Volume = $\pi(4.4)^2(5) = 96.8\pi$.

Step 4

1. **B** Plug in a multiple of 3 for x because element B is three times shorter than it. Try $x = 9$. That makes the half-life of element $B = 3$ and the half-life of element $C = 7$. Circle 7 and go to the answers. Choice A is negative. Choice B is 7, but remember always to check all five. Choice C is some fraction. Choice D is 2. Choice E is 31.

2. **J** You're told x is positive, so eliminate F and G immediately. Factor the equation to $(3x + 2)(x - 3) = 0$. The positive solution is 3.

3. **C** Plug in $m = 2$. Then it solves to $\frac{1}{4}$. Circle that and go to the answers. Choice A is out. B is $-\frac{1}{8}$. C is $\frac{1}{4}$. D is $-\frac{1}{4}$. E is 2.

4. **F** You can solve this in one of two ways. Plug in $x = 0$ to get $-\frac{1}{3}$. Circle that and go to the answers. Choice F is $-\frac{1}{3}$, and so is K. Plug in again: $x = 1$. Then you get $\frac{1}{2}$. Choice F still works, but so does K. Plug in $x = 2$ to get $\frac{1}{7}$. Choice F works, but K doesn't. Or you can factor the bottom to $(x + 2)(5x - 3)$ and cancel—whatever works better for you.

5. **A** Try them all in the equation (plug in the answers). Only A works. Don't reverse x and y.

6. G   Plug in some values. Because a couple of answers mention $d = 1$, be sure to try that. When $d = 0$, the value is -1. When $d = 0.5$, it's -0.75. When $d = 1$, it's 0. When $d = 2$, it's 3. It just keeps increasing.

7. C   Plug in $p = 2$. The new length is 6, so the area is 36. Check the answers. Choice A is 4. B is 12. C is 36. D is 144. E is 196.

8. K   Plug in $x = 10$. So Thad scored 10, 8, 35, and 21 points. His average was $\dfrac{74}{4}$, or 18.5. Check the answers. Choice F is 66. Choice G is 69. H is 2.5. J is 13.5. K is 18.5. Plugging In is great!

9. E   Well, the price went down, so eliminate A and B. Now plug in the answers. Start with D. Twenty percent of 116 is 23.20. Subtract that and you get 92.80. Too small, so the answer is E.

10. H   Try all the options in the equation (plug in the answers). Be careful to use parentheses on your calculator, so you don't make a mistake with the all these negative values. Only H works in the equation.

11. A   Plug in the values from the answers. Start with an easy one, like $y = 2$. The equation becomes $\sqrt{2(2)^2 - 7} = 3 - 2$ or $\sqrt{8 - 7} = 1$. That's true, so eliminate C and E, which don't include 2. If $y = 8$, the right side of the equation is negative, which can't be the result of taking a square root. Eliminate B. Plug in $y = -8$ to get $\sqrt{2(-8)^2 - 7} = 3 - (-8)$ or $\sqrt{128 - 7} = 11$. This is true, so the answer is A.

12. K   Plug in 2 for x. Choice K works out. You could also use FOIL to multiply them together. If you got F, you probably added the terms.

Step 5

1. **D** *k* is going to be determined by the factors of 12 that are used when this is factored. So what can you multiply to get 12? The sums of those numbers will be the possible values of *k*. 4 times 3 works, and they add up to 7, so B is out. 6 and 2 get rid of C. 12 and 1 get rid of E. –3 and –4 get rid of A.

2. **F** Follow the rules of exponents and you'll be fine. You always want to avoid negative exponents, so both *k* and *l* will need to be in the denominator. This allows you to eliminate everything except F.

3. **C** Straight proportions. Choice A is way too small, so eliminate it. Set it up like this:

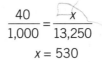

$$\frac{40}{1,000} = \frac{x}{13,250}$$
$$x = 530$$

4. **H** Plug in the value you are given and watch the negative signs. There's no need to cancel things first.

5. **E** In a function problem plug in the given value (–1 in this problem) everywhere there's a variable: $2(-1^2) - 3(-1) + 1 = 6$.

6. **K** Solve like an equality but flip the sign when you divide or multiply by a negative.

$$-\frac{3}{2}x + 2 > -1$$
$$-\frac{3}{2}x > -3$$

$x < 2$ (note the flip)

7. **A** Another proportion. Set it up like this: $\frac{120}{2.5} = \frac{x}{0.75}$ and solve for *x*. (These are real towns, but the distances are made up.)

8. H You've got to factor this. The minus at the end tells you it will look like this when done: $(x -)(x +)$. But how does it get split up? You need to find factors of 10 and 6 that will multiply together to give a difference of 11. For 10, start with 2 and 5. For 6, start with 3 and 2. Can you multiply these to get a difference of 11? 2 times 2 is 4. 5 times 3 is 15. The difference between 4 and 15 is 11. Aha! Now put it all together. You want a positive 11, so put the 5 and 3 in so that their product is positive: $(3x -)(x + 5)$. That leaves the 2 and 2. The final factored form is $(3x - 2)(2x + 5)$. So the solutions are found by solving $3x - 2 = 0$ and $2x + 5 = 0$. The solutions are $\frac{2}{3}$ and $-\frac{5}{2}$, which add up to $-\frac{11}{6}$.

9. C To be correctly factored, it must be broken down as much as possible. Pull a $3a$ out of everything and then factor what's left.

10. H Plug in or factor the top. It factors to $(a - b)(a + b)$.

11. C Go slowly and watch your signs. The first step is $8\left(-\frac{1}{2}\right)^2 = 8\left(\frac{1}{4}\right) = 2$. The next step is $-4\left(-\frac{1}{2}\right) = 2$. So you have $2 + 2 + 3 = 7$. If you didn't get that, you made a mistake with the signs or the fractions.

12. H The first equation should solve to $z = 5$. If you picked J, you didn't read the question correctly. Slow down. If you didn't get 5 from the first equation, you need to slow down.

13. D You could try to factor this, but plugging in 1 for q is probably easier. This leaves you with A and D. Try 2 or –1 and only D still works.

Step 6

1. D Break it up into smaller shapes. Draw a horizontal line to make a nice rectangle on the bottom. That rectangle is 20×22 and has an area of 440, so the total for the whole figure must be more than that. Eliminate A. Break the top chunk up into two triangles and a rectangle by drawing vertical lines down from the two top corners. Because the top of the remaining chunk is 10 and the bottom is 22, the bases of the two triangles must be half of the difference, or 6 each. But what's the height of each triangle? They're right triangles, so you can use the Pythagorean theorem or simply recall that 6-8-10 is one of the Pythagorean Triples that comes up all the time. So the height is 8. That makes the area of the middle rectangle 80, and of each triangle 24. $440 + 80 + 24 + 24 = 568$.

2. H Tangent is opposite over adjacent: $\dfrac{1}{\sqrt{3}}$. Multiply by $\dfrac{\sqrt{3}}{\sqrt{3}}$ to make the denominator a rational number.

3. C This is asking about the circumference of a circle: $C = 2\pi r$. The radius is the length of the pipe.

4. F Use the Pythagorean theorem: $a^2 + b^2 = c^2$.

5. B The slope formula is $\dfrac{y_2 - y_1}{x_2 - x_1}$. Just plug in the points.

6. G This is asking for part of the circumference. The whole circumference is 37.70 (see the explanation for question number 3 if you forgot the circumference formula). You want from 2 to 4 only, though. That's $\frac{1}{6}$ of the whole clock (draw it if you don't see this).

7. B First, find the slope by putting it into the $y = mx + b$ form. You should get $y = \frac{5}{3}x + 2$. Perpendicular slopes are negative reciprocals. The reciprocal of $\frac{5}{3}$ is $\frac{3}{5}$. Make it negative, and you have B.

8. G Sketch a little right triangle and use the Pythagorean theorem.

9. A You need to find factors of 144 that have a difference of 10. Trial and error with your calculator is the best approach here. 18 and 8 are the magic numbers. You can also use PITA to solve this problem.

10. H Split it up into two triangles, top and bottom. Each triangle has a base of 22. The height of one is 10 and the other 20. If you've forgotten, the formula for the area of a triangle is $\frac{1}{2}bh$.

11. D Draw a picture of the triangle. If $\overline{AC}$ is the hypotenuse, then angle B is the right angle. Sine is opposite over hypotenuse, but the hypotenuse is 10, not 5. Double the value given for sin A to $\frac{8}{10}$, and label $\overline{BC}$ as 8 and $\overline{AC}$ as 10. This is a 6:8:10 triangle, so $\overline{AB}$ is 6.

12. J First rearrange the original line equation by solving for *y* to find the slope. It's 2. For perpendicular lines, you want the slope to be the negative reciprocal of the original line. Rearrange each of the answer choices to see which one has a slope of $-\frac{1}{2}$. Only J does.

Step 7

The World's Fair Passage

1. A The opening sentence refers to its "peculiarities." Only "ironic" fits.

2. J In lines 23–24 it says that "each stood at the cusp between two historical epochs," which is a nice paraphrase of this answer. Although most fairs lost money, that's not mentioned as something special about these two.

3. A It's not stated directly. In lines 8–9, the Chicago attendance is given as 38 million. In line 15, Texas has 7 million. In lines 20–23, New York and San Francisco are described as having fewer attendees than Chicago.

4. H The nude ranch of paragraph 5 couldn't be described as "unimaginative," "realistic," or "timid," so "ambitious" wins.

5. B See lines 36–39.

6. J You want the one that's NOT true here. Choice J is contradicted at the end of the first paragraph.

7. C See lines 11–14.

The Drawing Passage

1. **D** In paragraph 8 she says that these artists see in a "special way."

2. **G** Read paragraph 2. It answers this directly.

3. **C** She says that you go into a "different subjective state" (line 92). That's not A or B. It could be D, but artists aren't sleeping.

4. **J** The phrase "deciding you shouldn't take a French class because you don't already speak French" is clearly silly. She's making the point that you can study things you don't already understand, art included.

5. **B** See lines 113–118.

6. **F** Toward the end of this paragraph, in line 85, she specifically mentions the right side of the brain—definitely a specific area.

7. **C** She actually describes these things as being the same. See lines 76–79.

8. **G** This is stated directly in line 110.

9. **A** This is emphasized throughout the passage.

10. **F** You can find a paraphrase of this in lines 88–95.

Step 8

1. **B** Check each of the answers and don't confuse the lines on the graph.

2. J Anthropogenic emissions always increase, so F is out. Choice G is also out, because there can't be a relationship between something that doesn't change and something that does. Forget H, because the increases of atmospheric mass don't match up with the temperature decreases.

3. A In the introduction, anthropogenic is defined as "man-made," so you can then just read the graph. It always increases.

4. H The temperature drops follow eruptions, so II is correct. The graph of temperature is also following that of atmospheric mass, so III is correct as well.

5. C This is a Why? question. Choice A is silly—volcanoes spit stuff out; they don't suck it in. Choice B may or may not be true—it's impossible to tell. Choice C makes sense because CO_2 is emitted but not absorbed into the atmosphere, so some CO_2 is missing. Choice D is irrelevant.

Step 9

Passage I

1. A Read the table in experiment 2.

2. H The best way to test a hypothesis is to experiment with it. If you want to test the effect of thermal conductivity, you need to experiment with a bunch of stuff with differing rates of thermal conductivity. In the intro, it says that the thermal conductivity depends on the material.

3. D Look at the table in experiment 2 and figure out where this bar would fall.

4. H Only difference in temperature matters, and the difference between 0 and 2 is 2, so find the answer with that difference.

5. B Also based on the table in experiment 2. As length increases, heat transfer rate decreases, so it's got to be B.

6. J If the temperature is the same all the way through, how could any heat flow?

Passage II

1. B What is something both of them say? Both describe light's behavior as wave-like. Choice A is in the corpuscular theory. Both C and D are only in the electromagnetic theory.

2. H The wave theory says that luminescent ether is undetectable. That would make it pretty tough to test.

3. D Choice A is in the electromagnetic theory. Choice B is in the wave theory when it says light bends. Choice C is also in the wave theory.

4. G An assumption is something that must be true for the theory to work. If light can't exist in a vacuum, that would directly contradict what the electromagnetic theory says about light's speed.

5. A The corpuscular theory says that light moves only in straight lines, like pool balls. Bending is out.

6. J If X-rays are the same as light, as the question is saying, then just replace the word "X-rays" with the word "light" in each answer. Choice F comes from the wave theory. Choice G comes from the corpuscular theory. Choice H comes from some medical journal and has nothing to do with this passage.

7. D Low frequency means high wavelength, so that's red.

Step 10

The Zoo Essay

High-scoring essays will vary in content and style, but we've included a sample of a high-scoring essay written in response to this prompt so you can get an idea of what to shoot for. See how closely your essay measures up to the one below in terms of length, structure, use of examples, evaluation of multiple perspectives, and command of language.

Almost all of us have memories of going to the zoo as children, either with our families or on school trips. Many animal rights activists believe that animals should only be put in enclosures in rare circumstances, and others believe the practice is inhumane for any reason. However, the experience of seeing a wild animal up close and personal can be both awe-inspiring and educational. I believe that as long as zoos provide a clean, safe environment for the animals, the benefits to both the animals and the public outweigh any negatives.

For many, abducting animals from their natural habitat and confining them in cages is a barbarous act that should be reserved only for when the survival of the species is at stake. Due to widespread poaching and deforestation, many unique and vibrant species are on the cusp of extinction. Zoos can reverse this process by placing endangered animals into safe enclosures, where they are protected from poachers and predators, and so have a better chance of successfully breeding. Many endangered species, including the white rhino, have recouped their numbers through such breeding programs. But while many animal rights activists believe endangered animals should be returned to their natural habitats after breeding, I believe the best way to protect threatened species is to ensure they have a continued presence in zoos.

Breeding programs are a necessity for endangered species, but at the same time, the long-term survival of all species depends on the enthusiastic support of the public. The best way to motivate people to make environmentally friendly choices is to remind them in a visceral, immediate way what exactly is at stake. As a kid, my favorite section of my local zoo was the bird sanctuary, which housed birds ranging from tiny sparrows to huge, red macaws. One day, a zoo instructor told us we should use cloth grocery bags instead of plastic ones, because many birds strangle themselves on plastic bags. I was horrified to imagine any of the sanctuary birds dying in this way, so I convinced my family to use cloth bags from that day on. By providing such interactive, educational experiences, zoos cultivate in their visitors a deeper appreciation for animals and a fierce desire to protect them.

However, zoos can only provide these positive experiences if they properly care for their animals. While it is clear from our society's acceptance of slaughterhouses and meat eating that animals aren't guaranteed the same individual rights as people, they should still be protected from abusive or neglectful housing situations. There have been several instances of animals starving to death in their zoo enclosures as well as predators escaping and consuming other animal residents. Such poorly run facilities not only undermine the safety and comfort of the animals but also instill negative values in in their human visitors. Instead of teaching children to nurture and cherish animals, these zoos teach them it is acceptable to confine animals in horrendous conditions for people's amusement. To ensure that zoos live up to their ideals, animals should be able to enjoy clean enclosures that closely mirror their natural habitats.

Well-run zoos may be the best chance to preserve the great diversity of animal life on our planet. While some might view animal confinement as inhumane, I believe this viewpoint fails to appreciate the wide range of services zoos provide, including protecting endangered species and educating the public on conservation. Until deforestation and poaching are eradicated, we need zoos to provide a sanctuary for the animals', and our, future.

About the Author

Shawn Michael Domzalski came to The Princeton Review in 1991 while living in Taiwan and working as a Chinese-to-English translator. He has received letters of recognition from both ACT and the California Department of Education for recording a perfect score on the ACT (something he's done at least eight times). He currently lives in Los Angeles with his wonderful wife, Danielle, and his furious cat, Cat. If you are using this book to improve your ACT scores, he suggests you stop killing time reading the author's bio and get back to the job at hand.

NOTES

NOTES

NOTES